JEREMY HOWE was born in south London and
now lives in north London having crossed the Thames
after living in Bath, Oxford, Belfast, York and Colchester.
He moved around because he used to be a theatre director
but now works for the BBC. He is married with two
grown-up daughters. mummy*daddy* is his first book.

Jeremy Howe

mummy*daddy*

PAN BOOKS

First published 2011 by Pan Books
an imprint of Pan Macmillan, a division of Macmillan Publishers Limited
Pan Macmillan, 20 New Wharf Road, London N1 9RR
Basingstoke and Oxford
Associated companies throughout the world
www.panmacmillan.com

ISBN 978-0-330-54392-7

3 5 7 9 8 6 4 2

A CIP catalogue record for this book is available from
the British Library.

Typeset by CPI Typesetters
Printed and bound by CPI Group (UK) Ltd, Croydon CR0 4YY

Visit www.panmacmillan.com to read more about all our books
and to buy them. You will also find features, author interviews and
news of any author events, and you can sign up for e-newsletters
so that you're always first to hear about our new releases.

With all my love to Jennie, Jessica and Lucy.

And Lizzie.

To protect the privacy of certain people
who collided with the car crash that was our life,
some names have been changed.

On the evening of 25 July the students for the 1992 English Literature Open University Summer School gathered in a junior common room in the University of York to be welcomed by their course tutors and to hear a lecture on the poetry of Stevie Smith from one of their teachers.

Welcomes having been given, the only thing missing was the academic who was supposed to be delivering the lecture – Dr Elizabeth Howe, BA (Oxon), M.Phil (London), D.Phil (London). She had been spotted soon after her arrival at the campus just after lunch and the course convener thought her non-appearance was strange. Eventually he went up to her room accompanied by a college porter and after repeated knocking on her door they decided to enter.

What they found there was her mutilated naked body. There was blood splattered everywhere. There was little doubt that she had been murdered. Dr Elizabeth Howe, Lizzie, was my wife and the mother of our two children, Jessica (aged six) and Lucy (aged four).

This is our story.

1

Do you find that birthdays and anniversaries come in waves? My mother, my father-in-law, my cousin and my godson all have birthdays in the first week of September, the same week that Lizzie and I got married, a week when I am supposed to buy cards and presents and – being a man – invariably forget half of them. That said, my family – the Howes – mark such days with serious intent, so imagine what the early summer is like for me: our youngest, Lucy, was born on 18 May, her older sister, Jessica, on 9 June ('June Nine,' she used to say in the broad Belfast accent she sported until she was three) and their mother – Lizzie – was born on 28 June. It is a kind of bomb alley for my poor bank balance.

That summer of 1992 was no exception; in fact, it was worse than usual, because we had decided to bite the bullet and have the kitchen in our small but lovely Oxford terraced house torn down and doubled in size. The work was due to start the week after Lucy's birthday and finish a couple of weeks after Lizzie's.

Lucy was four. She was looking forward to her birthday party big time.

Pre-school parties always start at three on a Saturday afternoon and finish at five and, like grief (only marginally less traumatic), have seven phases.

Phase one is getting ready. Of course getting ready is preceded by a week of planning, and then on the morning of the party you open the bedroom curtains with trepidation. This Saturday was going to be a beautiful day, but like that traditional summer pastime of exam-taking, the impending party is making both Lizzie and me edgy. We were not natural hosts and we took our party-throwing seriously: would the games (my responsibility) be up to the mark? Would the cake (Lizzie) pass muster? Were our parsimonious party bags going to elicit raised eyebrows from the mums? Would the guests behave, or, worst of all, would they just be bored?

After a ridiculously early supermarket shop, which fills the car with mostly crisps, and an equally ridiculously early lunch, the children are sent upstairs to get ready and/or mither around playing. The house is vacuumed by me to within an inch of its life (God knows why, considering the maelstrom that is about to be meted on it by both children and builders), Lizzie inspecting my work while she frets over the food, the birthday cake and what the girls would wear. 'Why bother with sandwiches when all the hordes want is cake and chocolate biscuits?' I say. Lizzie, who is a food puritan, and is at that moment cutting up carrot and celery sticks, gives me a contemptuous stare. As a concession to Lucy's birthday, she has permitted me to buy two bottles of Coke, which are to be handled as if we are letting the partygoers loose on vintage Champagne.

The birthday cake was more problematic. The year before Lucy had set her heart on a cottage (having been bargained down from an elephant or Flounder from Disney's *The Little Mermaid* on the grounds that they far exceeded her mother's cake-baking skills), but the cake had been a disaster, at least in Lizzie's eyes. Clearly she would have had problems if she had become an architect – her charmingly rustic sponge cottage would not stand up and had to be supported by flying buttresses made of chocolate swiss rolls. Lucy had been delighted with it, particularly the chocolate props, but the public unveiling of it in front of the mothers had been humiliating for Lizzie. So this year it was a simple one-layer sponge, decorated to look like a pond adorned with four marzipan ducks, one for each of Lucy's years. It is more naive art than neo-realism, and I reckon that the ducks looked quite duck-like myself, though Lizzie is not so sure. The idea was flagrantly ripped off from a neighbour of ours (a fine artist), who six months previously had delivered an epic, table-sized cake mapping out Treasure Island for her toddler son. Eating this work of art was almost as sacrilegious as the thieves who'd stolen Edvard Munch's masterpiece *The Scream* and had threatened to eat the painting if their ransom demands were not met. Lizzie couldn't wait for Lucy's friends to make her far less accomplished work of art disappear for ever. Between us we could muster four degrees, two from the

University of Oxford, and a full deck of very highly graded A levels, but we had both dropped art long before GCSEs, to concentrate on our studies, we told ourselves, but in fact because we were plain rubbish at drawing. No one ever told us then that to be a good parent you needed to be able to bake a cake or, even worse, design one.

But if Lizzie was in her own personalized hell of cake-making, I was matching it in struggling over preparing the games. Past experience told me that pin the tail on the donkey (just how do you draw a donkey?), pass the parcel (crucial to have a small gift secreted in each layer, I've always thought), musical statues and a treasure hunt would use up all of ten minutes and leave the guests in a state of frenzied excitement even before the promised feast of Hula Hoops, Kit Kats and E-numbers pushed their energy levels and grumpiness into the stratosphere. And just what music do you choose for musical bumps? Not too slow, not too fast, and probably not Lynyrd Skynyrd.

And then disaster strikes. Lucy, who now that she is four has decided it is high time she learnt how to slide down the stairs on her stomach, manages to give herself a nasty carpet burn on her cheek. She is inconsolable because it hurts; we are inconsolable because it looks like we'd walloped her across the face. I think my abiding memory of the party day is of Lucy dressed in all her party finery, sitting clutching her *Little Mermaid* toy, Flounder, watching a video with a big red mark on her cheekbone.

Of course the party is a breeze: five of the remaining

phases – the arrival of guests, the giving of gifts, the playing of games, the birthday tea and the mums arriving to collect – all passed by like a well-practised ritual. The cake goes down a storm; the children love the games (mostly because the Games Meister, i.e. me, is the most competitive person in the Western World, who, having missed out on his vocation as England manager, rules the jumping and running fest with an iron rod that makes the Fabio Capello regime look mimsy); no one cared that the party bags were miserable and cheap because the ten pence worth of sweets in paper bags were masked by the ingenious trick of getting the children to decorate their own bags after their tea; and NO ONE was sick before the mums arrived.

Phase seven is collapse – but not, of course, until after Lizzie and I had thrown away industrial quantities of half-eaten sandwiches, licked chocolate fingers and heaps of discarded carrot sticks, and then blitzed the wreckage that was our sitting room.

And then we have a treat to look forward to. Because both Lizzie and I had been working so hard (me at my job at the BBC, where I had several days' leave to use up; Lizzie masterminding the completion of her about-to-be-published book) and our Easter break had been totally screwed by my getting tonsillitis, we tell the children that tomorrow we are going to get up early and go to the seaside for a couple of nights.

Because I have a paranoid fear of traffic jams, we get up at the crack of dawn, load the car and drive to Swanage, where we had booked an expensive hotel (by our standards) sitting on top of a cliff with steps right down to a sandy beach. Given that the sun shone constantly and that we spent most of the day on the beach building sandcastles to stop the tide coming in (something dads love doing – and sometimes the children help), Jessica and Lucy had a whale of a time. So did I. I had not been to Swanage since my parents took me on holiday there when I was four years old. It had been the best holiday ever: we went by train – *first class* – from Waterloo, me dressed in my brand new school uniform; we stayed in a hotel, for me the first time ever; and I thought the Isle of Purbeck, with its sandy beaches, its high cliffs, its boat rides to the Tilly Whim caves and the finger-like ruin of Corfe Castle perched on its hill, was just holiday heaven. And when I return with Lizzie, Jessica and Lucy, I find that I know my way around Swanage as if I had visited it only a year before.

Having been to the National Trust shop, where Jessica, Lucy and I secretly bought their Mummy a lovely white and blue birthday mug with a drawing of a cat on it – we had just acquired a kitten in the hope that she would scare off the mice who were infesting our house, so cats were the girls' new obsession – Lizzie and I sit in a tea garden overlooking Corfe Castle while the girls go off and play. We chat about how fast they are growing up and I remark how familiar Swanage feels to me, how much of an impact it had made on me aged four, and I wonder how much of this little holiday will stay with our two, especially Lucy, who is now the same age I had been when I had first visited. As we leave to drive home, the dramatic ruin of the castle comes into sight once more, and I tell the girls to turn round and wave it goodbye through the back window of the car. I am consciously trying to create memories for them – a movie of their lives, in the same way that the Swanage holiday was like a Super 8 film recording my incredibly happy childhood. And as I try to piece together and understand what happened to us next, that moment has stayed with me.

Of course, what actually happens to us next is that the builders move in, which gives us a brilliant get-out clause for Jessica's birthday party three weeks later. We decide – sod the expense – to hold her party on a local farm.

Now, this is great – we could excuse the flamboyance (don't forget the Howe puritan streak I mentioned) because our house is a wreck and, apart from writing the cheque, all we have to worry about is the weather and the day living up to Jessica's mounting sense of excitement.

Well, the weather is iffy – a typical overcast Oxfordshire day, threatening showers – but once we have assembled the posse of a dozen children and a few hanger-on mums, for all Jessica cares it could have rained locusts: she is going to have a great time. We start with a treasure hunt round the farmyard, which involves the children meeting the cows, the chickens, the sheep, the pigs and the farm dogs. This is followed by a ride in a hay trailer pulled by a tractor. This may not sound exciting, but clinging on for dear life as the tractor roars its way along at about 10 mph up impossibly steep hills and back down again is about as exciting as it gets when you are six, especially as the farm dog, with a wonderful sense of being the party host, chooses to sit by Jessica for the whole trip. The children are far too excited to eat much of the birthday picnic in the hay barn – climbing and jumping off hay bales and playing hide and seek is too much of a distraction. And the invitations had baldly said, 'No Party Bags', so Lizzie and I, having achieved a local triumph with our DIY bags at Lucy's party, are let off the hook for this one.

On the way home Jessica wearily sighs, 'That was the Best Party EVER!'

'What was the best bit?'

'All of it!'

'Mummy, when can I have my party at the farm?'

'Next year perhaps, Luce.'

'Can't it be sooner?'

'Not really, darling, no. You've just had your birthday party.'

'Oh yes. I forgot.'

Two down, one to go. The weekend before Lizzie's birthday we go for a family picnic on a punt with John and Helen, two friends from college. It is idyllic. I have bought an expensive birthday cake in a tin (my reasoning being that a cake in a packet wasn't good on a boat), but never dreamt that we would need a can opener. While John and

I spend most of the picnic attacking this impenetrable tin with a penknife, Lizzie and Helen point out to the girls the difference between the coots and the moorhens on the river and throw the few crumbs of cake that we have painfully extracted from the tin to the ducks. It is also the week before Lizzie's book is to be published. She had turned her doctoral thesis into a narrative history of the impact that the introduction of actresses had had on the English theatre at the time of the Restoration of Charles II. The fairy godmother to both the thesis and the book, and the surrogate godmother to both our girls, was the superstar academic Inga-Stina Ewbank, and for Lizzie's actual birthday we decide to invite her and her husband Roger to supper. Because we couldn't cook (the kitchen again, but I should confide at this point that Lizzie was not a great cook and I was plain lousy in the kitchen), we take them out for dinner. It is one of those perfect summer evenings – celebrating a birthday and a momentous life-changing event that all of us are sure would kick-start Lizzie's halting academic career. Lizzie is the only person among all our combined families, friends and peers who has written a book that is to be published. She was relieved to have completed it, and I was so proud of her. Things couldn't really have been any better for us that summer of 1992 – Jeremy, Lizzie, Jessica and Lucy.

So who were the Howes?

Lizzie was born in Bradford on Avon in Wiltshire in

1958. Her younger sister Louise was born in 1961. Their parents, Ethel and Mirko Milicevic, known as Maka and Deda (Serb for grandma and grandpa and pronounced 'marker' and 'dayder'), married in Belgrade, where Maka – straight from school in Westbury, Wiltshire, and who had never travelled abroad before – was working for the Foreign Office. Because she didn't enjoy living there (once she married and went 'native' her security clearance at the British Embassy was downgraded; in effect, she was demoted to clerking) and he, as a middle-class Serb, was struggling to get on in Tito's communist state, they came to England. The man who granted Deda a six-month exit visa told him that if he reneged on it he should consider himself a dead man. Deda, who had no intention of doing anything but stay in England for good, ignored the visa, and so didn't return to Yugoslavia until that man died some fifteen years later. Begrudgingly, Maka's father got Deda a job sweeping floors at Bowyers Sausage Factory near Bradford on Avon, there not being much call for Serb trained lawyers in Great Britain. A few months into the job his supervisor told him that if he played his cards right he would make foreman in five years. By the time I met Lizzie, both the girls had been through private education at Bath High School, they had a grand house, and Deda was the International Development Director for the company who had bought out the company who had bought out Bowyers.

I was born in 1956 in Bexleyheath – in Kent, so called,

but in fact an entirely anonymous suburb of London – the middle one of three children, Jonathan, Jeremy and Philippa. My father – who died in the late autumn of 1991 of just about everything – ran a small cloth merchandising company in the West End that had gone belly up during Edward Heath's three-day week, which had left us in penury for much of the seventies. Ironic, as he was a lifelong supporter of our constituency MP, one Edward Heath. The situation was not helped by my mother walking out on him (he was a nice man, but was also a workaholic, absentee father who never said much – I could see her point) and for four years we lived apart, he with his mother in Teddington, the rest of us in Bromley with my mother's mother in a vast house that we rattled around in because we didn't have any furniture. It was owned mostly by my aunt, my mother's sister, who was always threatening to move in, which is another reason why we left half the rooms uninhabited.

Growing up in a single-parent family was an adventure – all the rules of family life had changed; we were in a new place leading new lives with brand-new friends with whom I never talked about my dad not living with us ('Oh, he's away right now'), and my mother seemed to treat life as if we were on some permanent summer holiday. I learnt to be a very self-sufficient child and I learnt a lot, unconsciously, about single parenting. I also worried constantly on my mother's behalf about money, because we never had any. We were middle-class poor.

But my father was a stubborn, dogged individual, and he put the marriage back together. Suddenly, thank god, the ramshackle, seat-of-the-pants, no-money life was over. One weekend all five of us went into town and my father bought a new fridge, so we didn't have to use one shelf in my grandmother's refrigerator. Never had the purchase of a domestic appliance brought such joy to a thirteen-year-old boy – it was a sign that we were destined to be a family again.

Four years previously, at the start of the summer holidays, while we drank squash in the garden one morning, my mother had said, 'Jonathan, Jeremy and Philippa, I have some news. We are going away this summer, first for a week in Norfolk and then we are going to move house – to Bromley.'

'Really!?'

'And your father is not going to come with us.'

'Not on holiday, Mummy?'

'No, when we move to Bromley,' she said solemnly.

'Why not?'

A question she never really satisfactorily answered.

Now, as casually as they had appeared to separate, they came together again.

'Your father is coming to stay.'

'For the whole weekend?'

'No. For good.'

*

By the time of his death, my parents' marriage was as near perfect as a marriage can be. Even so, I never really got on with him, mostly because he never spoke. They were both lower middle class and had both left school at sixteen. But they were upwardly mobile, so when their two clever sons both got exhibitions to the University of Oxford they were dead proud of us. They upped sticks from London and moved to Sudbury in Suffolk shortly after I went up to Oxford.

That is where Lizzie and I met. We both studied English, were in the same year, and shared a love of theatre. She never remembered the first time we actually met, in a mutual friend's room with about six other people; I did. She sat in a corner on the floor in a perfectly splendid fur coat she had picked up for a song in the Oxford market. But we met properly when she stage-managed a production of Samuel Beckett's *Endgame* that I was directing, rehearsing all through the Easter vacation of our second year. As stage manager, she was ruthlessly efficient, totally reliable, well organized, hardworking and unfailingly nice to work with. She had also agreed to share a flat with me and my best friend (who was playing the lead in the play) for the following academic year.

After the show had finished, the cast and crew all went their separate ways, as is the way in the world of theatre, swearing to meet up and of course never doing so. Except, one afternoon I dropped by the workshop where my designer – Jim – was building a set for another show. Lizzie was there. In fact, I kind of knew she would be, which is probably why I went. I walked in unannounced. I remember her standing with her back to me, one leg crooked in her skin-tight jeans and incredibly trendy Kickers shoes, one hand on her hip and one hand holding a paintbrush. Her long chestnut hair cascaded down her back. She was upbraiding Jim for faffing around and he was teasing her. When I said hello, she turned round, smiled at me, said she had to go or she would be late for a tutorial, and left.

'I saw the way you were looking at her. Jeremy Howe you fancy Lizzie Milicevic something rotten. You just want to get inside her pants Mr Howe!'

I went bright red and muttered something incomprehensible. Jim was right – but I hadn't realized it till that moment.

It was the spring of 1978 and we started going out together a couple of weeks later. We started living together about a month after that, and I think we knew this was the one from that moment on. She worked hard for finals, but never panicked. I just panicked. Of course, she had worked steadily throughout her time at Oxford, whereas I had more or less taken the second year off, so I had good cause to panic. We both got a viva for a first – the moment I opened my mouth in mine, I am sure the examiners realized I was a sham who knew nothing but could write a good essay, so I didn't get a first. But nor did Lizzie, who was so obviously a first-class student in brains, in academic ability and in application. It rankled with her for ever. Her cause wasn't helped by the fact that when she got nervous or excited her brain would work faster than her mouth and she stammered, which I found endearing, and she hated.

We graduated and moved to London, where I tried and failed to get work as a theatre director and she puzzled over what to do next. In retrospect, it was blindingly obvious she should be an academic, but at the time she was unsure. She did a masters degree in Restoration theatre, which she didn't much enjoy, then worked in publishing in Brighton, before setting up a social research journal at York University that led her into hospital administration and what looked like a promising career. When we moved to Colchester she was offered a similar job, but she threw it all in to do her doctorate and paid her way by teaching at a crammer in London.

When we moved to Belfast she started teaching for the Open University – most interestingly at the Maze Prison, where she taught a former hunger striker who was the most gifted student she had ever come across. After we went back to England and settled in Oxford, she got down to turning her thesis into a book, while still doing some teaching. *The First English Actresses* was published by Cambridge University Press just weeks after Lucy's birthday party (and it's still in print – easily available from Amazon for just £26.99). It immediately got a rotten review in the *Sunday Times*, but then, months later, all the academic journals started reviewing it – fulsomely. It won an award in the States, it was turned into a stage play (going to the first night, I was so proud my heart all but burst), was reviewed on Radio 4's *Woman's Hour* and later was the source book for a not very good movie. And it is still making money. So much for the *Sunday Times*.

You might be wondering why Lizzie's short life reads like a round-Britain road movie. The answer is because she was following me, of course. After a year of doing nothing in London (I sold screws and glues at Selfridges), I got my break as a theatre director at York Theatre Royal, where my three-month contract somehow lasted three years. And one morning in February 1981, just before I left for York, while I was shaving in the bathroom and she was getting dressed in the bedroom of our tiny flat in Bayswater, I suddenly called out:

'Lizzie, why don't we get married?'

So we did, in September 1981, from her parents' house in Bath. It was a wonderful Indian summer day, but it wasn't just the weather. It was the wedding itself – weddings are the most beautiful public way of celebrating a relationship. And the honeymoon in Venice wasn't bad either.

It was the only occasion I can remember that Lizzie wore heels – and she didn't like the photograph of us coming down the aisle of the church with her towering half an inch over me. In bare feet she was as tall as me – which isn't saying much, as I am only five foot eight (and a half). Lizzie Milicevic was now Lizzie Howe – she hated her Serb name, which made her stand out when all she ever wanted to do was to blend in. Her foreignness fascinated me, but to her it was an irritant. A conversation in our early courtship went something like this:

'Hello, I am Lizzie Milicevic.'

'Hi, I'm Jeremy Howe.'

'That's a nice name.'

'Jeremy?'

'No, Howe. Will you marry me?'

'Er . . .'

'So I can change my name.' And she grinned.

And on 5 September 1981 we were both grinning with sheer happiness.

But our lives were complicated – Lizzie had to stay in London for her research and I was in York. We both lived in digs at opposite ends of the country and most of our quality time was spent at the buffet in King's Cross station. We were not happy. When Lizzie got the publishing job in Brighton, I moved there to be with her. But no sooner had I done that than my work dragged me back up north. So she chucked in her job and we moved into a beautiful house on the Fulford Road in York, opposite the police station.

After York, I got a job in Colchester, where we bought our first house. Then my career went pear-shaped – the theatre there nearly went bust and I was laid off. We had been trying for a baby without success (her idea, not mine), and for a year Lizzie was taking fertility drugs. 'If nothing happens this time, I think we should bring in your husband for a sperm count,' said the consultant, baffled by his patient's inability to conceive. A few weeks later Lizzie had arranged to meet me in town for lunch immediately after her latest appointment with the doctor. I was waiting on a street corner when she came up from behind, tapped me on the shoulder and whispered in my ear, 'No need for the sperm test, sweetie.' Jessica was on the way. Only problem – I was a freelance theatre director, which is an arty euphemism for being unemployed. 'You need to get a proper job, Jeremy,' Lizzie said forcefully. I had under nine months to find one.

In January 1986 – with less than five months to go – I was interviewed for two posts: one to run the theatre in leafy Farnham in Surrey, the other to work for the BBC as a radio drama producer in less leafy Belfast.

Both interviews went well and I had high hopes.

A week later I was offered one of them. Of course, I couldn't wait to tell Lizzie, who was teaching at her crammer.

'I've got the job.'

'Brilliant. Which one?'

'Er . . . Belfast.'

'Oh fuck.'

The Troubles were still at their height, so her reaction was perhaps not all that surprising. In fact, we moved to Belfast a couple of weeks after our neighbours in Colchester – the Royal Anglian Regiment, some of whose appallingly drunken behaviour made Colchester town centre a no-go area every Friday night – went on a tour of duty to Ulster.

A fortnight after the move, at five in the morning, Lizzie, by now heavily pregnant, woke me up.

'Jeremy, I'm bleeding.'

'I'm sure it's nothing serious. Go back to sleep, darling. Don't fuss.'

'No, I'm bleeding. Look it up in Penelope Leach. Now.'

I stumbled out of bed, found the motherhood and childcare book, looked up bleeding and pregnancy, where it said, reasonably unambiguously, 'IF VAGINAL BLEEDING OCCURS IN THE LATER STAGES OF PREGNANCY GO TO A HOSPITAL IMMEDIATELY.' Or words to that effect.

The ambulance arrived ten anxious minutes later, and Lizzie spent the next month in hospital suffering from placenta praevia. The consultant reassuringly told me that 'If it is between saving the mother's life or the baby's, we save the baby's.'

Jessica was born two weeks prematurely by emergency caesarean section on 9 June 1986. We had no problems at all conceiving Lucy, who was born naturally on 18 May 1988. Even more astonishingly, Lizzie had researched most of her doctorate while she was pregnant with Jessica and wrote it between Jessica's birth and Lucy's, less than two years later. Supermum. She even had to go for the viva with the baby in tow. Her supervisor minded Lucy while she was examined. Fifteen minutes into the examination – an interview with three eminent academics – the Academic Chair said, 'I think someone out there needs you more than we do. Congratulations on getting your degree, Dr Howe, I think we should all go and look after the baby now.' And out they all trooped to a wailing Lucy.

A year later I got a job at Film 4 and we moved back to England after three very happy years in a war zone. Mortgaged to the hilt, we could just about afford a small family house in Twickenham. On the way there from Bath to look at possible houses, Lizzie said to me, 'Do you want to live in Twickenham?'

'No.'

'Nor do I.'

So we failed to board our train, went back to her parents' house and came up with Plan B. We moved to Oxford, and I commuted to London every day. Every bloody day, from our lovely little four-bedroomed terraced house, garden back and front, less than a mile from the city centre and the libraries Lizzie needed for her research, within walking distance of two state nurseries, 400 yards from the River Thames on one side and water meadows on the other. Commuting apart, it was brilliant. 'I never, ever want to move again,' said Lizzie, and she didn't.

After a couple of years I rejoined the BBC, as Editor of Drama on Radio 3, where I was working in the summer of 1992. Life seemed pretty good.

Like all relationships, we had our ups and downs, but I think we both knew in our hearts that we had found the right person with whom to share our journey through life. We were sure in each other, and like many of the strongest couples we knew, we had grown up together. Not far from where we lived was a place called Wittenham Clumps, two trees on a hilltop commanding a view over the river below (where we would go to play Pooh sticks) and across the Thames flatlands to the distantly gleaming spires of Oxford. Lizzie and I were Wittenham Clumps – one tree faced east, one west, each protecting and supporting the other, and the more we grew, the more we counterbalanced each other. As a couple, we were greater than the sum of our parts – the two of us sharper, more dynamic, nicer, better, stronger, richer than just Lizzie or just Jeremy.

And Lucy and Jessica?

Two beautiful, lovable girls.

Jessica, now six, was quite tall for her age, boisterous, loud and brimming with innocent confidence. My abiding image of her that spring was her sitting at her little desk in the bay window of the bedroom she shared with Lucy, writing her book, while her Mummy wrote hers in the study next door. The first time I saw her as a newborn baby, wrapped in swaddling clothes and handed to me by the midwife, she fixed me with a steely, blue-eyed stare which rather implied, 'Who are you, exactly?' She has maintained that gaze ever since, inquiring and accusatory. Although inclined to be bossy, she doted on Lucy. They were the very best of friends and playmates.

Lucy was little and four. It's odd to think that this slightly chubby, small individual has grown into a taller woman than her sister. She was the exact counter to Jessica, with whom she got on wonderfully, but boy could they quarrel, especially when Jessica's tendency to be overbearing got to her. Lucy was shy, quiet (well, I think 'silent' is the technical term), biddable and had a very sweet nature that masked a quiet determination: Lucy always knew her own mind, it's just that she didn't really feel the need to share it with anyone else.

Three birthdays done and dusted, one book successfully published and a new kitchen – we Howes were ready for the summer holidays. All we had to do was negotiate Lizzie's week away teaching at the Open University Summer School.

2

And so on Saturday 25 July 1992 we all got up to start the summer holidays.

The girls had broken up from their school round the corner a couple of days before. As an end-of-term treat, they had all been asked to turn up in Victorian costume to celebrate the hundredth anniversary of the school buildings, where a beautiful stained-glass window made by a friend of ours was unveiled. It was a day of intense excitement, and the pictures that a neighbour took of them in their Victorian bonnets and long frocks (well, two of their mum's not-so-long dresses hemmed up) are incredibly cute.

For Lizzie, the Friday had been a day of anxiously putting the finishing touches to the lecture on Stevie Smith that she was giving the next day to kick off the Open University Summer School at York.

I had had a day from hell at work – clearing my desk for a week's holiday is always a nightmare of unfinished business and decisions that have been put off being hastily made – but it was compounded by an event the previous evening. An elderly actress had just dropped down dead during a play recording. Apart from a lot of legal health and safety shenanigans, it had left the production team in a state of shock, and I was trying to dispense some much-needed TLC. Almost as bad, the recorded rushes of a programme had completely disappeared off the face of the planet, which was like pissing a sizeable programme budget down the pan; I had to find out what had happened. I had arrived at my desk at some ungodly early hour and finally left to go home at about eight that evening. For a bit of light relief, I took a producer out for lunch whose last day it was in the BBC, after a career of some forty years. John was from Alexandria, a Greek anglophile who had grown up under English rule in Egypt; he was one of the most urbane, cultured and wise men I had ever met in the BBC. Over coffee, I asked him what the best play he had produced was. Without hesitation, he said, 'The one I have just completed. Yeats's version of *Oedipus* has more wisdom than any play I have encountered.'

'Why?' I only vaguely knew the play.

'The last two lines are extraordinary. "Call no man fortunate that is not dead. The dead are free from pain." In other words, no man is happy until he dies.'

'That's pretty bleak, John.'

'Ah, but don't you see – he was living in dangerous times. I think what he means is that we just don't know what is round the corner. What is to come. That you cannot rest on your laurels until the moment you die. Very sobering, don't you think? After all, none of us knows what lies ahead.'

'Oh, I know what lies ahead. My bloody in-tray is waiting for me.'

Saturday dawned as a classic first-day-of-the-holidays morning – sunny and cool, but with a promise of hot weather to come.

As I shaved and she vigorously scrubbed her teeth to the reassuring tones of the Radio 4 *Today* programme, Lizzie and I joked about David Mellor and the infamous Chelsea strip.

'What an arsehole.'

We were in a tearing hurry – Lizzie had to be on a train to York first thing, then I had to do the packing and take our newly acquired kitten, Milly Molly Mandy (named by Jessica – don't ask), to the cattery before Jessica, Lucy and I hit the road for a week. We were driving to York to meet up with Lizzie via my mother's house in Suffolk and my sister's in Norfolk, all rounded off with a weekend on the beach in Scarborough: the kind of rigorous route march of a holiday I specialized in. Because I was anxious about what to do with the children when in sole charge, I had concocted a timetable that would keep us on the move until we hooked up with their Mummy on the Friday afternoon.

We raced to the station, just a little bit late, snatched a not very nice breakfast at the buffet, and then trooped to the platform to await the train. As it drew in, Lizzie arranged to phone me from a payphone at about six (mobile phones were few and far between in 1992), just before I had planned to leave for my mother's. We said our farewells, doors slammed, porters larked with the mails and, with the train drawing off, we waved goodbye. We waved and waved as if our lives depended on it, until the train slowly disappeared round a bend. Our family. Lizzie, Jeremy, Jessica and Lucy.

I shepherded the girls off the platform, acutely aware of a sense of anticlimax – the train had departed, the station was quiet but for the cheeping of the sparrows in the eaves of the station roof, and while Mummy was off to do her glamorous job in an exciting place, we only had the prospect ahead of a day of domestic tasks. I felt myself to be faintly heroic in my herculean task for the week – sole carer for the children. What a saintly husband I was. God knows how I would get through the week.

It was a frantic day, as I simultaneously packed, looked after the children, supervised the electrician who had come to finish off our brand-new kitchen and drove the kitten to the cattery. This involved a mere thirty-mile drive with a screeching animal, while the children played with their best friends across the road. Lizzie didn't phone at six o'clock. But what with feeding and bathing the children ('Tonight I am cooking pizza, girls!' Straight out of the packet, with juice and carrot sticks and a sliced apple for dessert), I didn't notice that she hadn't until I was halfway to Suffolk, with the children dozing in their pyjamas in the back of the car. As I thundered along the motorway I watched a plane take off from Stansted airport and, when it banked, the whole fuselage glowed like burnished copper as it caught the rays of the setting sun, and I wished we were on it, going on holiday to some beach, and then I thought of Lizzie and felt vaguely annoyed – there she was, having a good time at the summer school and forgetting us, and here was I, with two sleepy girls en route to see my mum on a boot camp of a holiday.

We arrived in Sudbury and though I managed to greet my mother, recently widowed and in her late sixties, who hovered by me wanting to help, I just brushed her aside as I raced into the house and went up to the attic bedrooms with sleeping children in my arms, first Jessica and then Lucy, who woke up and, with a sleepy smile, hugged me tight and fell back to sleep. The sweet smell and intense warmth of my sleeping children brought a sudden rush of parental love. I stood them up and took off their dressing gowns and slippers, as they tried to ask what time it was. They rubbed their eyes, clutched their teddies and, as I lay them down and pulled the blankets up around them, Jessica said, 'Daddy, I love you,' and then, like Lucy, she was fast asleep once more.

I raced back downstairs, unloaded the car, and then at last gave my mother a hug.

'Has Lizzie phoned?' I asked.

'No, darling. The only person I have spoken to this evening is Philippa.' My sister.

'That's odd. That's not like Lizzie. I wonder if she has forgotten to take your number with her to York. I wonder when I'll get to talk to her.'

'She's probably having a good time and has forgotten.' Lizzie was so punctilious about such things that I thought it unlikely, but we sat and chatted about the girls, what my mother had planned for our long weekend with her and all the Sudbury gossip, me with a beer and my mother with a cup of tea, and before long I had forgotten about the missed call. Knackered, I went early to bed.

I am aware that I am having an anxious dream when I wake to find my mother in her dressing gown standing over me, shaking me.

It is pitch-dark.

'What's the matter? What's the time?'

'Darling, there is someone banging on the front door and shouting that he is the police looking for a Mr Jeremy Howe. It's one o'clock.'

I wake instantly. I gather myself together, register the knocking that had been invading my dreams, and pad downstairs as fast as I can, my mother following me like a shadow.

I open the front door a crack.

'Are you Mr Jeremy Howe? May I come in?' It is a young police constable. Looks about twelve.

'Yes. I am Mr Jeremy Howe. What's the problem?' I

wonder if he wants me to move my car as I think I might have parked it on a yellow line outside the house, and I feel disgruntled.

'It's about your wife.'

'Is she OK?'

'I am afraid she has been injured. Can I come in please?'

'How badly injured?' I ask as he stands on the pavement and I stand in pyjamas.

'Can I come in please?'

He comes in.

I shut the door.

My mother stands anxiously behind me wringing her hands.

'How badly injured?' A whole sequence of scenarios about nursing her back to wellness race through my mind, which is abruptly halted by—

'She is dead, sir. You need to phone this number. It is a direct line to the officer handling the case at York police station.'

Shit. I can't have heard him correctly.

'Dead? Lizzie dead. That's not possible.'

'I am afraid she is dead, sir.'

I wasn't expecting that. I WAS NOT EXPECTING THAT.

Call no man fortunate that is not dead.

Suddenly I am very awake.

'She was attacked. You'd better phone this number, Mr Howe.'

I see Lizzie lying in a ditch, bleeding. How on earth would Lizzie have got into a fight?

I phone the number, speak to a very matter-of-fact Yorkshireman, who tells me that my wife had been found dead in her room on campus at about six o'clock on Saturday evening, that her throat had been slit, and that they had apprehended an Open University student on the York campus at about eight o'clock who they will charge with killing her later today. It appeared to be a random attack in the middle of the afternoon by a man, tanked up on vodka and drugs, whose life had come off the rails, and who had never met Lizzie before. Instead of killing himself, he had killed her, or so the policeman thought. She was the wrong person in the wrong place at the wrong time. Luckless. She was one of the most blameless people I'd ever met. And now she was dead. Not dead – murdered. There was no way of turning the clock back to the moment about five minutes ago when I'd had hope (Lizzie had only been hurt), or ten minutes ago when my life had been normal. Shit. This was BLOODY HOPELESS, and there was no one to bargain with, no one to retrieve our lives, no one to wind the clock back. As I listened to him, I found myself thinking, 'So this is how it was meant to happen.'

As if what had just occurred was inevitable.

'So what should I do now?' I ask.

'Well, Mr Howe, we would like you to come to York to identify her body. We would like you to come as soon as possible.'

'How?'

'I suggest you don't drive yourself, Mr Howe. You will be in no fit state to drive.'

'Er . . . well, how do you suggest I get there? I'm in Suffolk. It's the other side of the country.'

'By train.'

'On a Sunday? I won't get there until the evening.' I expected him to say that someone from the Suffolk police would drive me.

'Get a friend or a relative to drive you up.'

'I'm with my mother. She doesn't drive. What should I do?'

'I am sure you will manage. The earlier you come, the better, Mr Howe.'

'OK.'

'We really are very sorry, Mr Howe.' I can hear the noise of the police station in the background – people chatting to each other in hushed, businesslike tones with Yorkshire accents, radio traffic, the clack of typewriters, the sound of a distant normality, like the soundtrack to a radio play. It seems simultaneously so close and yet it seems as if it comes from another planet.

I put the phone down. I don't know what to do. I don't know how to react. What are you supposed to do at the moment when your life implodes?

I stand there and say to no one in particular – 'Lizzie – has – been – murdered.' I see the policeman standing there embarrassed, my mother looking helpless.

I just don't know what to do or how to react, so I collapse onto the floor and sob. I can feel the hard stone floor beneath the rug which is getting damp as I weep. I taste the carpet's bitter wetness in my mouth. I hear my mother asking the young police constable if he would like a cup of tea.

'No thanks. I'd best be off.'

I feel a bit silly, so I stand up, wipe away the snot, blow my nose and apologise for my behaviour. We shake hands and he takes his leave.

My life is changed, and I don't know what to do.

I think of Lucy and Jessica innocently asleep up in the attic.

I don't know what to do.

After a cup of hot sweet tea, my mother and I make a plan. Even though it is nearly two in the morning I phone my sister who is outwardly calm and tells us to come to Norfolk once the girls are up. She sounds like she knows what to do, which is more than I can say for either of us, so her plan becomes our plan. I try ringing Lizzie's parents, but the call goes straight to an answerphone message. I try a dozen times, but with no success.

I still don't really know what to do, so because it is the middle of the night I go back to bed, but I can't sleep. I go to my mother's bedroom. She can't sleep either. I lie on my mother's bed, on top of the covers, she hugs me and we talk – about Lizzie, and about Lizzie and me, and how happy our lives have been, how we met at Oxford and how falling in love changed me as a person, our struggles in London, our crazy lives apart in York and Brighton, but how that strengthened our love, our struggle to have children, and so on and so on, but my mind is in turmoil. I can't engage with anything, I can't focus and eventually my mother goes back to sleep and I try to doze beside her. It is as if I am a child again.

Shortly after four I give up trying, get dressed, and not knowing what else to do I creep out of the house and go for a walk across the water meadow on the other side of the street.

The world is grey and colourless. A drizzly mist hangs over the riverbanks, cattle graze silently, their snorting breaths breaking the silence, but that apart, nothing is stirring. The world may just be waking up, but I am wide-WIDE awake. I am wired, I feel giddy with emotion, I want to run, I want to shout out, I can feel the loss of Lizzie like a sharp pain in my stomach, I feel like my head should explode with the sheer enormity of working out how to understand what has just happened. I feel smashed up. I want to be alone. I want to tell the world. I want to take Lizzie in my arms and tell her I love her. I want to kill the man who has done this to her, to us. I feel terrible that I can't wake the children and tell them. I feel terrible thinking about what I am going to have to tell them. I so want to talk to Lizzie. I want to talk it through with her more than anything in the world.

I have never felt lonelier. I haven't felt like this since

before I met Lizzie. I am alone. Alone in a new and frightening world.

I walk fast, because I am thinking fast. It is as if I want to run away, but run away from what? From myself, from my life as it has just been reconfigured? Actually I am thinking clearly and quickly, as if my life depends on it.

I walk for about half an hour or so, working through options. Do I stay in Oxford, do I move to live with my mother, or with Lizzie's parents in Bath or with my sister Philippa or with Lizzie's sister, Louise? Do I relocate to London to be nearer to my job? Do I ditch my job and bring up the children? How should I bring up the children? By myself? Or do I just bury myself in work and get one of my family to bring them up? What do I do about work? Surely I can't go back to work? Or do I look for a new mother for the children? Where do I look? Or do I just run away and travel round the world and try and find myself – with or without Jessica and Lucy?

As I walk, I come to the footbridge across the Stour, a typically sleepy lowland English river, a river made famous by the paintings of John Constable. Nine months earlier I had stood here on a cold, clear starlit night trying to digest the news that my father had just died. That night I looked at the stars laid out above me and thought, hey, his death, upsetting though it was, was just a part of the order of things, the universe shifting, recalibrating. I felt sad, but there was a natural justice in his death, his life had been of the right span. But not Lizzie's death. Her death

– her murder – is an outrage against nature, the news of it smashes like a steam hammer through any idea I might have of a harmonious universe. All I can feel is hurt, anger. The injustice of her death is a physical pain – my heart is beating fast, my breathing shallow. I can feel the blood pressure building up in my brain. My stomach is in knots. I want to scream, I want to hurt something. I rub my furrowed brow trying to relieve the stress, trying to think clearly. And the river flows on, forever and ever, the cow by the bridge stares at me, chewing and snorting, its tail swishing to a regular beat.

I walk on.

There is a fork in the path. I hesitate. Turn left and I return directly to my mother's house, turn right and I loop right round the meadow, over the river and head home that way. Left or right? If I go left I sink, if I go right I swim. Left or right? Sink or swim? Do I let myself drown, let this destroy me? Onwards? Or downwards? I am frightened. So frightened. I want to be sick. I take several deep breaths, I try to clear my head, to push my panic to one side.

Christ, this is for real.

What would Lizzie want me to do? What would Lizzie *have wanted* me to do? With each second her life was coursing away from me like the water in the river beside me.

I take the right fork.

I swim.

I will endeavour to bring up the children as best I can, I will keep my job, I will maintain our lives. I will move forward.

I will do what I think Lizzie would want me to do – bring up the children as best I can, keep my job, maintain our lives, move forward.

I hold my head. I stand up straight, breathe deeply and stride forward.

This is not going to be easy.

I will swim.

In that half-hour walk, I made most of the decisions about how to lead my life, our lives, which is the story of this book. For years, if I have needed to clarify what I am doing and why I am doing it, I have tried to get back to the state of mind on my walk through the Sudbury water meadow. It is my Mount Sinai, and Jessica and Lucy are the tribe that I will lead out of the wilderness.

The first step along that path was to go to my sister's, who had offered to look after Jessica and Lucy while her husband Malcolm drove me to York to identify my darling Lizzie's body.

I crept back into the house, through the garage door and into the kitchen. My mother was standing with her back to me, her hand clasping the kettle while she waited for it to boil. She was lost in thought. She turned round and, as she did so, I saw her face change from anxiety to warmth, as if she had put on a mask. She smiled at me and gave me a hug.

'What shall I say to the girls?'

'I know. Worrying about it woke me up. I just don't know, darling.'

'Suppose that Lizzie isn't dead? Suppose they have got the wrong body?'

'I know.'

'I just don't know what to do.' I had no idea what to say to them, or how to say it.

I poured two glasses of juice – just as Lizzie and I had done every morning. I went upstairs and even though it was not yet six o'clock, I woke them up.

'Darlings, there has been a change of plan. We're going to get up now and drive to Auntie Philippa's before breakfast.'

'Why, Daddy?'

'Er . . .'

Pause.

'Something has come up. Daddy has to go to the office. With Uncle Malcolm.'

Not one of my best fibs, but they were excited about seeing their Auntie Philippa and their cousins Jennifer and the twins and their dog.

'Will we go to the seaside, Daddy?'

'Not today. Maybe later in the week.' And they accepted their Daddy's gloss on the day. But I had bottled out.

I just wasn't ready to tell them, so we began to live a lie.

Off we set, with the girls in the back of the car, still in their pyjamas, all snuggled in blankets and dozing, with my mother in the front. The grey, drizzly dawn had turned into a grey, drizzly day. The windscreen wipers washed away the rain, but they did not wash away the tears. At each traffic light, at each road junction, I surreptitiously wiped my glasses, hoping that the girls did not see what a state I was in. My mother affected not to notice that I was weeping almost constantly.

We arrived at my sister's sometime around eight o'clock; under heavy grey skies everything felt muted. It was as if I was wrapped in cotton wool. We talked quietly in corners, in case the children overheard, we had breakfast, and I made the phone call I was dreading.

Still Maka and Deda's phone went straight to a machine.

What to do? I phoned directory enquiries and got the phone number of Maka's best friend and neighbour. I knew her, but not well.

'Sue, it's Jeremy Howe, Lizzie's husband. I am so, so sorry to disturb you so early on a Sunday.'

'I've been up for hours. No worries.'

'I have to get hold of Lizzie's mum and dad. It's urgent and their phone goes straight to the answerphone. I have to talk to them as soon as possible.'

'I see.'

'Would you do me a favour and go round to the house

and get them to ring me on this number immediately. It is not good news.'

'Of course. Right away.'

Five unendurable minutes later the phone rang. I could hardly bear to lift the receiver.

'Maka. Thank God. I have been trying to get hold of you all night.'

'Bloody Deda. Put the phone on answerphone. I don't know why he has to mess about the phones. Wretched man.'

'I have some terrible news.'

'Yes,' she said calmly but breathlessly.

'Lizzie has been killed.'

'I see.'

Pause.

'How did it happen?' she said, just as calmly. I told her and she responded as if she had been expecting this to happen for a long time. 'I see . . . I see . . . yes . . . of course . . . of course.'

I put down the phone. Silence. I tried to imagine what Lizzie's mother was doing at that moment. In my mind, I heard an anguished howl, saw a face cracked open with sobbing, her husband unable to console her tears, then or ever.

I made calls to her sister Louise and to my brother Jonathan, to break the terrible news to them, to the police to tell them I was leaving, and then I breezily said goodbye to the girls, who were busy admiring my sister's doll's house with their cousins, and set off with Malcolm on my awful odyssey to identify Lizzie's body in York.

3

I was the worst passenger in the world.

I was in limbo. Strapped into a kind of spaceship traversing the rolling plains of eastern England on a journey into unknown territory. A mission with a purpose, but God knows what purpose. My mind was either in freefall or was blank because I could not comprehend what I might be about to face.

We drove in silence. Malcolm – twelve or so years older than me, Welsh, a research engineer for the Lotus car company, well paid, hardworking, very clever, but not a talker – suggested, 'You never know, it might not be Lizzie. You won't know until you have identified the body.'

There was a 1 per cent chance of this being the case. But Malcolm was right: there was still a scintilla of hope.

As we got closer to York – and I began to recognize places Lizzie and I had known from our three years there – a knot tightened in my stomach. I got fidgety and nervous. The kind of feeling you get before the opening night of a play, when you know you are going to have to go on stage, but you have no idea how well you will perform.

I was on a different planet to the one inhabited by

everybody else. Planet Grief is an alien place, smashed up, desolate, savage, but strangely compelling. So this is what it is like to be King Lear on the blasted heath. He on his pilgrimage to Dover to try to find redemption, me to York to find God knows what. I was trying to make sense of the mess, but there was no sense to be made. It just was. All I could do was try to stand up in the howling gale that was buffeting me and embrace the storm, not fight it, nor reason with it. It must not destroy me.

I was in the first phase of grief – shock and disbelief.

Inside the car, all was quiet, the landscape, at last lit by the sun, pastel and beautiful, like an English watercolour. And although my heart was racing, my head pounding, my jaw locked with tension, I was sitting still. Although I was wrestling with emotions I had experienced only in studying Shakespearean tragedy, I could be distracted by the boy coming out of the newsagent unwrapping his Mars Bar, the dog squatting by the lamp post, his owner trying to look the other way as the animal defecated. Life went on in that Sunday morning way.

We stopped at a Little Chef ten miles or so short of our destination for me to go for a pee. I didn't want a pee, but I did want to delay our arrival, delay having to confront the truth about Lizzie. There was still hope. Once I had identified the body, there would be no hope – and in my heart I knew that was what was awaiting me. I felt sick.

We arrived in York sometime before ten, and parked in the empty hospital car park, all too familiar from when I used to meet Lizzie when she had worked there as an NHS administrator eight years before. The sun shone in that hard, bright, heatless way it does in the north. We walked over to reception, a vast, empty cavern, shut up for the weekend. The Assistant Coroner greeted us, shook our hands – 'I am sorry to meet you under such terrible circumstances.' He was tall, in his fifties, grey, charming, wearing a tweed jacket, was softly spoken and very apologetic about everything he asked us to do.

He led us quickly down spotless white corridors, through doors, down steps, round corners, into the centre of a deserted maze, until we reached a large room suffused with daylight from above and divided in two by a long, diaphanous white curtain covering a glass partition.

'This way, Mr Howe,' and he took me behind the curtain while Malcolm waited in the lobby.

There is a gurney covered in a shroud. There is a body beneath.

'Are you ready, Mr Howe?'

My God, it is happening so fast. Five minutes ago we were parking the car and now I am in this unfamiliar room whose boomy silence will stay with me for ever. It is like the moment of take-off on an airplane when the hours of waiting end, as suddenly, with a roar of engines, the plane hurtles you into the skies. Am I ready to confront the unconfrontable? No, but none of us is ever ready: I can't believe this is happening to me.

He pulls back the cover.

There is Lizzie.

Or the body of Lizzie. It is the woman I had kissed goodbye barely twenty-four hours ago, but lifeless, and not Lizzie at all. She doesn't even look like Lizzie sleeping, but like someone who resembles her. Apart from a livid red mark on her throat she doesn't look like she had been either hurt or traumatized.

'Mr Howe, is that your wife, Elizabeth Howe?'

'Yes. It is. It's Lizzie. It is Elizabeth Howe.'

What happens now? Would we just go home?

'Mr Howe, would you be prepared to make a statement to the police to that effect?'

'Yes. Of course.'

'Mr Howe, I wonder if it would be at all possible for you to come down to the police station to make the statement. Everything's closed here because it's Sunday. It would be easier. And I am sure the police officers on the murder inquiry would like to meet you.'

'Of course.'

'Mr Howe, would you like a few moments alone, just to say goodbye to your wife?'

I hesitated. Yes, I supposed I should. But I was not sure why.

'Yes. OK.'

'Please don't move the sheet covering your late wife's body, Mr Howe'.

He closes the curtain to give me privacy.

I hear the mumble of Malcolm and the Assistant Coroner talking as I stand and gaze at Lizzie. At Lizzie's body. I don't know what to do. I feel self-conscious. I dare not touch her. I feel giddy. I think my heart is about to explode.

And then I start to weep. I weep and weep. I kiss her gently on the forehead, I tell her that I love her, that I promise to look after the children, I thank her for our lives together, for our love, our girls, our happiness. It is a nightmare, a *nightmare*, or like some ghastly film, but I am not acting, this is real, and I can't believe this is happening, and happening to me. I still can't believe this happened, that this waxy cold body, looking so calm and at such peace, is the violated body of the person I love with all my heart.

I say a prayer, a prayer I have said every night now for nearly twenty years.

'Dear Lord, thank you for Lizzie, please let her know that I love her and please let her know that I promise promise promise I will look after the children.'

And then despite my tears and an unendurable wrenching physical pain I pull myself together, say goodbye to her, and walk through the still white curtain and into an uncertain unknowable future, knowing only that I will never see Lizzie Milicevic, Elizabeth Howe, my heart's best treasure, again.

As if from a great distance I could hear the Assistant Coroner's voice.

'Will you come with me, Mr Howe?'

'Of course.'

'I suggest we drive in two cars to the police station – if you would follow me. Do you know York?'

'Yes. We used to live here. Lizzie and I.'

'It is just that the one-way system is impossible, and if you don't follow me you might get lost.'

We follow the Assistant Coroner to the police station. I know the way because our last house in the three years we had lived in York had been bang opposite. It was now a B&B, and we were booked in to stay there at the end of the week.

I am in a daze. We park and as Malcolm and I walk towards the entrance to the police station the Detective Chief Superintendent, in cap and uniform and holding leather gloves, ambles past and we are introduced.

'I am so sorry, Mr Howe, that you are having to visit this beautiful city under such awful circumstances,' he says as he shakes my hand.

'I know. We used to live here. It is a horrible homecoming.'

'Oh, I didn't realize.'

'Yes.'

'Thank God we have apprehended the man we think did this terrible thing.'

'Yes.'

'If there is anything you need us to do – like book a hotel if you have to stay, or anything like that – do let us know.' Thinking about it afterwards, I reckon that the Superintendent had probably been waiting in the car park for us to arrive. As he walks over to his car I have mixed emotions: I am confused by his offer of finding a place to stay, I feel like some toxic celebrity. I had never been introduced to establishment bigwigs like him before and I envy him as he gets in his car and drives off back to a life of normality I had just been barred from.

There was no way I was going to stay in York overnight. My intention was to leave the moment I had written the statement. It was now just gone eleven o'clock. We wouldn't get to leave until mid-afternoon.

The police told me that the man who had killed Lizzie had been arrested, dressed in her clothes, when trying to drive off from the campus in his car just as it was getting dark. They had apprehended 'her' because 'she' was behaving so strangely.

We go into the police station, a large, drab, uncared for 1970s building, buzzing with activity, and the Assistant Coroner leads us into the bowels of the station, past officers in shirtsleeves, walkie-talkies at their sides crackling with barked messages.

We walk past a table in the corner of a corridor and laid out there is the dress that Lizzie had been wearing when she had left home yesterday and there my briefcase ('JP Howe Form 5A' written on the flap, a gift from my parents for getting through my O levels) that Lizzie had always used: a glimpse of our domestic normality in this alien setting. I try to linger, but am hastily ushered into an airless cupboard of an office overflowing with files. The

Assistant Coroner fusses around with pieces of paper, and eventually unearths the correct form. 'Not my office, I'm afraid. Just one we use from time to time.'

He gets me to certify that I had identified Lizzie's body and sign it, and then disappears.

I sit with Malcolm in silence.

Fifteen minutes later, he reappears. 'The officers running the enquiry have asked me to get you to write something a little more detailed. Would you mind?' he apologizes.

'Sure. What kind of thing?'

'Just write down where you were and what you were doing yesterday from the time you last saw your late wife until the time the police contacted you at . . . when was it?'

'About one o'clock this morning.'

Ten hours ago.

'Until one o'clock then, if you'd be so kind.'

'OK.'

Pause.

'Where is the man who they think killed Lizzie?'

'Oh. He is in one of the cells down the corridor, I believe.'

'Has he been charged with her murder?'

'Not yet. By law they need to give him some rest before they are allowed to question him.'

Sitting within a few yards of the person who killed Lizzie was surreal. I want to kick the shit out of him, to stab him, to kill him. I want to retrieve her things sitting outside on the table, to touch them, smell them, steal them back. It would be so easy. I take a breath and ask if I could have them back, or at least go and look at them.

The Assistant Coroner gets defensive. 'No. I am afraid the police will need to use them as evidence. They shouldn't really have been there when you came through . . . Here is another form. Just fill in what you did yesterday, would you please? And if you don't have space, just ask for another piece of paper. Look, I'll leave you to it and see if I can rustle you up a sandwich. I fear all this may take time.'

I start to write on their form – a diary of what felt like my last day before we entered hell. I get to the bit about taking Milly Molly Mandy to the cattery, which Lizzie had booked, not realizing it was halfway to Swindon, and had been a real pain to find – and I had cursed her for it. That had been at about four o'clock, about the time they think she was murdered. Apparently, people along the corridor from her room had heard screaming, had called out, but the screaming had stopped, so they had assumed everything was alright. She had lain there dead for over two hours. I had been cursing Lizzie at roughly the time that she had died.

As I write the statement, I realize that Milly Molly Mandy is my alibi, and that if I need an alibi, then I might be a suspect. Do they really think that I might have been involved in the murder of Lizzie?

It is a thought I keep to myself.

I finish the statement, read it over and sign each page: I wonder what I am signing away. The Assistant Coroner thanks me. 'Can you hang on a while? I just need to show it to one of the officers on the case.'

We wait an age, in silence, and then a police officer pokes his head around the door. 'The Detective Inspector who is running the case just wants a few words with you. Would you come upstairs with me please, Mr Howe?'

I need moral support.

'Can my brother-in-law come with me?'

'Oh. I won't be a minute. I'll see if that's OK.'

Another age.

'Is that alright, Malcolm?'

'Sure. Sure.'

He reappears. 'Yes. Your brother-in-law can come too.'

We are led upstairs and shown into a very large room, which looks more like a study than a detective's office. There are sporting shields and such like on a bookcase. Two burly police men in plain clothes are standing waiting for me, and after the offers of condolences, which now feel ritualized, I sit down in a chair facing the desk, the Detective Inspector sitting facing me, the other to one side. I am aware of Malcolm, silent, just behind me. My back is to the large window which overlooks the house where Lizzie and I used to live. It had been our first home together, just the two of us. We had been very happy there.

They question me, taking it in turns – soft cop, hard cop.

They *are* treating me as a suspect. The worst day in my life has just got a whole lot more nightmarish. They ask me to talk my way through my statement, through my comings and goings the day before. When they get to my trip to the cattery they slow down, they want a minute by minute breakdown of what I had done, where I was, who could verify this information.

'Do you have the number of the owner?'

'Not on me, no. Sorry.'

This is serious. The Detective makes a note on his pad. Silence.

'And do you know a Robin Pask?' asks his colleague.

'No. Who is he?'

'Did he know your late wife?'

'Why?'

'We think he killed your wife.'

'I have no idea if she knew him. The name doesn't ring any bells with me. Not that I know of. Who is he? Lizzie might have taught him at the summer school before, I suppose. I wouldn't know.'

'He is a science student from Bolton, Mr Howe. Do you think your late wife might have taught him?'

'No chance. Lizzie taught English. Neither of us have ever been to Bolton.'

'Would he have any motive for killing her?'

'NO! Lizzie was blameless. Why would anyone want to kill Lizzie!?'

'Sounds unlikely that there's a connection there, I'd say. Any money problems at home, Mr Howe?'

'What do you mean?'

'Were you in financial difficulties?'

'No. Why?'

'People get their nearest and dearest killed to claim on the insurance.'

'My life is insured, not Lizzie's.'

'How was your relationship with your late wife?'

'What do you mean?'

'Did you get on? Did you quarrel?'

'Er . . . no – just normal stuff. We get on fine. We got on just fine.'

'How was your sex life, Mr Howe?'

'Er . . . fine. We have two children.'

'I mean, were either of you having an affair, Mr Howe?'

'What do you mean? No. NO!'

And on and on, twisting me into tighter and tighter knots. I feel under terrible pressure. I want to shout out, I want to make jokes, I want to tell lies, I want to tell them to fuck off. What right do they have to do this to me? Meanwhile, the man who killed Lizzie was sleeping in a cell so he was refreshed enough for police questioning, whereas I had been up since one o' bloody clock.

Finally:

'We would like to search your house in Oxford. Can you give us a key? Do you have one on you?'

Bloody hell. They are serious. I have the front-door key to Oxford in my pocket. I am sure there will be one in Lizzie's purse. We have a mate – Henry – staying there, house-sitting for us. But I don't want them ransacking my house without me being there. I reach breaking point.

'No. It is with my brother. In Hampshire. I don't have his phone number on me, I'm afraid.'

It is a lie. I can feel myself blushing.

They must know it is a lie.

There is silence while the Detective Inspector facing me thinks. He motions to his colleague and then says, 'No matter, Mr Howe. We don't think you were involved in your late wife's death. It would just be a routine search. Do you have any questions?'

'Yes. Who is he, Robin Pask?'

'Well . . . we haven't questioned him yet, but he's in his thirties, some kind of lab technician from Bolton, Lancs, an Open University student on his first summer school, is married, two kids. Has a previous police caution for threatening violence towards women – his neighbour we think – and he has a history of mental illness. As far as we can tell from the officer who arrested him, we think he got to York sometime around yesterday lunchtime. Got tanked up on booze and pills – vodka, speed, that kind of thing – and he appears to have randomly attacked your late wife. More than that, we don't know. We don't really know why he did it, I am afraid.'

The Detective Inspector says, 'OK, Mr Howe, you are free to go.'

'Thank you.' I stand up.

'What would you like us to put in the press release?'

Press release?

I sit down.

This can't be happening.

'Er . . . ?'

'Would you like a press conference?'

'Um . . . Should I have a press conference? I'm not sure – why would I?'

The two officers share a look. 'We generally only suggest the victim's relatives hold a press conference if we think they have something to hide. It flushes them out, if you see what I mean.'

As they are speaking I suddenly recall a recent news story. A dead girl's boyfriend had made a passionate appeal for her killer to give himself up at a police press conference. The next day the boyfriend was arrested and charged with her murder.

'And . . . do you think I have something to hide?' I asked.

'It seems pretty straightforward to us. Your late wife was the victim of a random knife attack by a complete stranger. So, no, we don't. Not really.'

So we drafted a press release, and then they said that if there was anything they could do, please get in touch, that they would stay in contact with me about the progress of the case, and they wished me well.

I couldn't wait to get out, to get some air, to retrieve some semblance of my life, to escape from this nightmare.

But before we started our journey home, I had one more task to perform.

I crossed the Fulford Road by the police station and

walked up the familiar garden path to the house where Lizzie and I had lived during our last year in York – the top floor of a beautiful Georgian farmhouse, right on the edge of the city, and now a bed and breakfast. I knock on the door. After an age it opens and a man looks at us quizzically. I have obviously woken him from his Sunday afternoon nap.

'Hello. My name is Jeremy Howe. We have a booking for my family – myself, my wife and our two girls – for next Saturday evening. Which I would like to cancel.'

'I see.'

'My wife has been killed.'

Silence.

'We have just heard. Just come from the police station.' I rather pathetically point to the police station over my shoulder.

'I am so sorry.'

And with that, we left for Norfolk, to pick up the pieces of my life.

4

The journey up to York had been like a mission into the unknown. I returned from there not with good news, but with ashes.

We turned on the radio to catch the news.

We were the last item of the three o'clock Radio 4 bulletin, whereas this morning it had not been mentioned. 'Police have arrested a man in York suspected of killing an unnamed Open University teacher.'

We retuned to BBC Radio York.

'Police have arrested a man in York suspected of killing a Doctor Elizabeth Howe . . .' and they read out verbatim the press release I'd co-written not half an hour ago.

The enormity of what had happened to me hit me afresh. It was unbearable.

Using one of those first-generation mobile phones the size of a brick, Malcolm called home to let Philippa know we were on our way. I briefly chatted with her. 'We've just got back from the summer fête in the next village. Jessica and Lucy had a lovely time. We've just settled them down in front of the video of Jennifer's ballet class. Do you want to have a word with them?'

'No. Just send them my love. But please please don't turn on the radio. The news is just breaking. I really don't want them to hear.'

'OK. When are you going to tell the girls?'

'I don't know, Philippa. I just don't know.'

I couldn't think what to say, so I just remained silent. I felt a million miles from the events she was describing in Norfolk – lunches and trips out and ice lollies and a day spent playing with the cousins. I was an eternity away from normality. I so wanted a lifeline to that world, and here I was returning, not even with ashes, but with a toxic virus: I was coming to blast the world that I so hoped would look after me.

Each mile seemed longer than the last. I desperately wanted to be home, but home for what? What was home now? Home had been us, Lizzie and I, we had built that loving home. Home was now me and God knows what. Going home should mean going home to share with Lizzie what had happened. All my adult life, that is what I had done. Now I was alone, I had no one to share the awfulness with, and now that the news was out, I could not put off telling the girls. But what was I going to tell them? How was I going to tell them? It would wreck their lives.

It was as if somebody had just plunged a knife into me, as if something had smashed my life into a million pieces. I felt lost. I felt sick with grief, and sick with fear. I wanted to cry. I couldn't cry. I wanted to scream. I couldn't scream. I wanted to blot out the future. I wanted to curl up and hide. I wanted to run away. I wanted to pretend none of this was happening. I wanted to go to sleep. I was like a boxer lying on the canvas after receiving a knockout blow, who is aware of the world beyond the ropes shouting and baying, but all he can think about is lying on the floor, barely able to hear the noise, he can just hear the blood ringing in his ears. I wanted to lie on that canvas for ever, to curl up in the car seat, wrap a blanket round myself and pretend that none of it was happening.

I was exhausted. I was wired.

I imagined never being able to sleep again. I wanted to sleep for ever.

'Well, you can take a sleeping pill,' suggested Malcolm.

'I don't have any sleeping pills. I've never had a sleeping pill. Ever,' I snapped. But the idea took hold of me.

Malcolm phoned home again.

'Jeremy needs sleep. Does anyone have a sleeping pill?'

My sister asked my mother. No. She had some in Sudbury. Philippa rang off, ransacked the medicine cabinet and phoned back. 'No, we don't, sorry.'

It became an *idée fixe* with me. Malcolm suggested we try a doctor. Good idea. But on a Sunday afternoon?

Malcolm played a game of telephone tag that progressed like a game of snakes and ladders – it was torturous, especially as I was a counter on the board rather than the dice-thrower. He phoned home to get them to call the doctor. The surgery was closed and there was no out-of-hours message. Malcolm didn't believe them, so he phoned the surgery himself and then phoned home and got the number of a friend of a friend who had the home number of the doctor, whom he then phoned. The doctor was out at lunch, but should be back shortly, which wasn't shortly at all, and Malcolm phoned home to let them know we had got hold of him, and then the doctor phoned, but the signal went down (this was 1992, harly anyone had mobile phones, calls cost roughly the same as a bottle of whisky, and nowhere in the country had much coverage), and then he phoned back. Malcolm explained to the doctor what was needed; the doctor suggested trying a casualty department. OK.

Nothing had been achieved, but it had filled an hour.

We then listened to the four o'clock news on Radio 4, and now that they had a name, they had a story: Lizzie's death was the lead item.

The phone rang. It was my sister saying that Henry – our house-sitter in Oxford – needed to talk to me. Why? She had told Henry what had happened. Why? Because there were about a million journalists camped outside our front door who wanted a comment from him – which he was refusing to give – and a photograph of Lizzie.

Oh God.

I spoke to Henry, and between his shocked reaction and my state of numbed grief, he managed to convey to me that if he could give a photograph of Lizzie to the press outside they had promised to leave us alone.

This was horrible. But I wanted to help poor Henry. I sent him off to hunt out the photographs that Lizzie's publisher had had taken of her just a few weeks previously. She'd hated nearly all of them, but I knew that there was one that captured her to a tee that she had liked. He found the photos in her meticulously tidy study and we talked through them. He described each one.

'No. Not that one.'

'There is a nice one of her in the garden smiling. I think it's a lovely likeness.'

'No. Not that one. She hates that one.'

'Hold on a minute. Someone's at the door.'

A pause. I could hear Henry's gentle Dublin lilt saying, 'Just a minute. Just a minute. Just be patient, will you? No you cannot talk to her husband.' And the front door shutting.

Our house in Oxford was under siege.

'They have a deadline,' he said to me. 'I said we would get them a photograph as quickly as we could. It's like a scrum out there. It's unbelievable. They won't take no for an answer.'

I rejected photograph after photograph as he described them to me over the phone. I finally agreed on the image of Lizzie that I thought was the one that she likes. The one that she *liked*. This was so important to me. And I got it wrong. Plastered across every newspaper over the next few days was a grainy image of Lizzie smiling that, once I saw it, I knew she hated – for some reason, her cheekbones look ridiculously high, and I can tell that the smile is more of a rictus grin than an expression of her natural warmth. Even now, I still feel wretched about agreeing to use that image. But as I rang off, apologizing to Henry for putting him in the eye of the storm, I felt like I had achieved something. But Malcolm saw how distressed I was.

'I will phone that doctor again.'

The doctor was reluctant, but Malcolm would just not take a no from him. He agreed to meet us at the surgery, and said that we were to phone him once we were back in Norfolk.

Of course, once we got to Norfolk, because Malcolm is a man, and men never go to the doctor, he had no idea where the GP's surgery was, and after another round of telephone tag we finally arrived sometime after six at a purpose-built health centre in the middle of nowhere, which was about as deserted as York General Hospital had been earlier that day. The GP, a tall man in his late forties, let us in after five fruitless minutes of us banging on glass doors and buzzing buzzers. He was clearly pissed off at having his Sunday interrupted.

He hadn't really believed what Malcolm had told him on the phone. He asked me to tell him in my own words why I was distressed, and as I relayed what had happened in the previous seventeen hours, I could see that if we had been in a sitcom his jaw would have dropped. I had never told a story before that had had such impact. He was appalled by each twist and turn of my terrible day and quickly granted me my wish – he fished out of the desk drawer a blister pack of twelve tiny blue bombs.

He split the pack in two. So furtive was the process, it was like meeting with a dealer.

I only ever took one half of one pill at a time, and somewhere in a drawer squats a spare half-pill.

It is easy for me to see my story from my point of view. Almost impossible to see or understand the collateral damage I was inflicting on others. What on earth was going through my brother-in-law's mind during our eight hours of driving? What must I have been like as a travelling companion? How was he reacting to the awfulness of the news? And as for the doctor – well, I kind of came into people's lives like some plague, like some inverted Midas, polluting everything I touched without even being aware of it.

5

We arrived back at my sister's.

The children had had their bath, were in their pyjamas and Grandma was reading them a bedtime story.

'Daddy, Daddy, look at what I got at the fête,' and Jessica showed me a bracelet that Auntie Philippa had bought all four of the girls.

'Look mine is green, Daddy,' chimed in Lucy.

'And Cousin Katherine's is purple!' and Jessica twirled her wrist to model her new fashion accessory.

'So you had a good day?'

'Oh yes! We had the best day EVER!' And Jessica gabbled away nineteen to the dozen about everything they had done since they had arrived at the cousins', but I was not really hearing her. All I could think of was that I couldn't tell them now. Not before bedtime. I just couldn't. I kissed them goodnight, I cuddled them and continued to live the lie.

'I shall tell them tomorrow,' I said to myself.

But, alas, tomorrow came all too soon.

After a night of drug-induced sleep, I crept downstairs at about seven o'clock on that Monday morning. My mother and sister were in the kitchen, talking in hushed voices, struggling to come to terms with our new shared nightmare lives.

Philippa wondered if I might do it when I woke them up, because she was sure that Jennifer – the oldest of her three children – had sussed that something was up. But as they were sleeping with their cousins (what a treat! Naturally, they didn't have a clue as to why we had been spoiling them rotten), I didn't think it was a terribly good idea. It was an excuse, of course. I wondered how long I could go on living this weird make-believe with Jessica and Lucy. Days? Weeks? Years? But the worry of it was making me ill. I had to act PDQ. But just how would I tell them? I needed a script to read them – I had been a theatre director, after all, and I always directed from a script! I could imagine the stage directions and then the first line ('Darlings, I've got some very bad news'), then I turn the page for the next line and it is completely and horribly blank.

I poured out two glasses of juice and took them up-stairs. I woke them up like Lizzie and I did every day.

'Did you sleep well, darlings?'

'Mmmmmm. Yes. Very. Daddy, I was having lovely dreams about dancing in a ballet with the cousins.' Jessica always wakes up wide awake and chirrupy.

'And you, Lucy?'

'I'm tired.' Lucy never wakes up wide awake and is never chirrupy.

'What are we going to do today, Daddy? Are we going to the seaside?'

'Not today. Another day perhaps.'

'I'm tired.'

'Did you talk to Mummy last night, Daddy?' asked Jessica.

Pause. An agonizing pause. It felt like I had been kicked in the stomach. I could feel blood rushing to my head, my throat constricting.

'I miss Mummy,' said Lucy.

A pause which felt ten years long. How much longer could I live this lie?

'Oh, sweetie pet.' I ruffled her hair. 'She sends lots and lots and LOTS of love.'

'When can we talk with Mummy?'

'Well, it's tricky because she isn't on the phone. Why don't you finish your juice and get dressed and then let's have breakfast and we can take a walk round the garden and we can decide what to do today.' I diverted them into thinking about what to wear and to getting dressed, and then I slipped downstairs, feeling like a soldier who had just been relieved from frontline duty in a dangerous trench.

My mother, sister and I decided on a plan.

Immediately after breakfast, I would take the girls into the garden and would tell them. My mother would follow after to help pick up the pieces, while my sister told her three in the sitting room. Not a particularly detailed plan, but a plan nevertheless.

Telling the girls was so painful that I am struggling to remember what happened next. I have blanked it out.

I can remember them eating their breakfast. I can remember saying to them that there was something I wanted to tell them and asking them to come into the garden.

'Is it about the holiday?' Jessica bounced. 'Are we going to the seaside today?'

If only.

I remember that getting to the garden took for ever, and I can remember exactly where we stood. Alongside a high cypress hedge. I remember how grey the sky was, how still the air, how humid. I remember crouching down to be on their level and putting my arms round their shoulders, thinking that I only had one line and then I didn't know what to say, but I have no memory of telling Jessica and Lucy that their Mummy was dead.

My mother said she could hear the low rumble of my voice, then silence, then an awful cry from Jessica, and she came running. My sister later said that wail was like the end of Jessica's childhood.

Jessica says that she remembers thinking, 'I wonder how long it will take the trees in the hedge to grow tall enough to reach Mummy in heaven.'

I don't really remember anything, except that when I said I would look after them just like Mummy had looked after them, Lucy wailed, 'But, Daddy, you can't cook.'

'Yes he can. He cooked us pizza on Saturday,' Jessica blubbed.

'But that was from a packet.'

'And he cooked us fish fingers last week,' Jessica wept.

Jessica then proceeded to list things that Daddy could cook. It wasn't an impressive list – Lucy had a point. She'd rumbled that I was clueless and under-skilled in the mother department.

6

That time in Norfolk with my sister was the strangest of weeks.

It was a week spent in limbo, as I moved from denial, the second phase of grief, to the third: pain and guilt. We grownups sat around, mostly silent, as if we were waiting for something to happen, while all the children played happily together. Every so often, Jessica or Lucy would come to me just for a hug, and then would resolutely scurry off to continue playing, while one of us would go and make a cup of tea or flick through a newspaper.

The papers were the first thing to absorb. You don't really expect to become a news story, but at the beginning of the school summer holidays, a couple of weeks after the horrific killing of Rachel Nickell on Wimbledon Common, Lizzie's death was headline news. On the Monday morning the photograph of Lizzie I had agonized over the previous day, and which I grew to hate, was plastered across the front pages of all the tabloids, and a bit more tastefully across the rest of the press. That it was a big story somehow vindicated my grief, but the coverage was so inaccurate and sketchy. I didn't really recognize the family paraded across the front pages as us. People whom I had never heard of in our street in Oxford said nice things about us, and the Open University – for whom she had worked for four years – clearly had no idea who Lizzie was. My boss was quoted as saying that I had had a glittering career in front of me. 'Had', note, not 'has'. On Friday I had been one of those upwardly mobile, thirty-something execs in the BBC with a promising future; by Monday, because of personal circumstances, I was washed up, a has-been. And thanks to my boss, all on the front page of a tabloid.

I phoned my boss to explain why I wouldn't be coming into work, to explain that I wasn't sure if I was ever coming back to work. Without pausing to think about it, he said that I shouldn't even consider returning until things had settled down, offered me all the support and love he could muster, etc., etc. I never mentioned his quote, but it was obvious from our conversation that he still thought of my job as in the present and not in the past, which was a con-solation.

I called Inga-Stina Ewbank. She was inconsolable. She said it brought to mind King Lear's dying speech. 'Never never never never never,' he cries over the body of the dead Cordelia. It is the most heartbreaking moment in theatre. When I put the phone down, I realized I was in that play, not as a bit-part player, but at the centre of the storm. I was high on a mountain, removed from the rest of the world, and just thirty-six hours ago I had been normal and a part of that world. It was as if the gods had plucked me from my humdrum happy life to test me.

Like ambassadors from the real world, two university friends of ours who lived in Cambridge visited on the Tuesday afternoon. While their girls played with my two, we sat in the garden. Karen – a journalist – was nursing their newborn baby.

She said the only way to put the press disinformation right was for me to do an interview: she knew just the person, someone at the *Daily Telegraph*. I called him later that day and he was very nice to me, very concerned. Just as he was ringing off, he innocently asked me where I was staying. I paused, and then demurred from telling him anything other than 'East Anglia'. I had kept the gate closed. My sister's house – a pretty cottage set in a large, beautiful garden in a secluded one-shop village in the middle of nowhere in Norfolk – was like a refuge from a storm. No matter how much the phone kept ringing – it was always for me, and it rang a hell of a lot throughout that week – the gates were closed, the garden was calm, and we could keep the outside world, which felt alien and not a little frightening, away from us. In this oasis of calm, I felt I could protect Jessica and Lucy and me from being exposed.

And yet, I confess, all this publicity made me feel good. I both wanted it and hated it. It made me feel needed; it made me feel important, that the awfulness of what we were going through was not as utterly pointless and existential as it felt like, that it was somehow validated by the outrage of the rest of the world. But I also lived in fear of being doorstopped.

As other news stories of the August silly season kicked in (it was the time of the Barcelona Olympics and, like John Major's hapless new government, our team were winning sweet F.A.; meanwhile, David Mellor and his family values were still being hammered by the press as he vainly clung onto office), Lizzie's death moved from page one to page three and then, by the end of the week, disappeared altogether. I felt cheated, but was gratified when the *Independent* ran an obituary of Lizzie, making the cherished life that I had lost sight of feel as significant as her death. OK, so it was written by Karen, but it made me so proud of Lizzie, helped me realize what an extraordinary person I had married.

Sitting in the sun-drenched Norfolk garden, Karen, her husband Andy and I had talked about damage.

'You don't need to be damaged by this, you know. You and the girls will be different, but you don't need to be damaged.'

I think Karen was right. I have taken enormous comfort from what she said. We are different, we have led a different life to the one we might have led if Lizzie had not been killed. Some things are less good, some things are better – we have had more adventures and my relationship with Jessica and Lucy is bound with hoops of tempered steel. The broken bone, a colleague said, is stronger once mended, and our bones are strong for having been broken and expertly reset. The only person who came out of it with nothing – and as I write this I am angry and upset and in pain as I ponder the pointless waste and loss – is, of course, Lizzie herself.

Family came and family went – Maka, Deda, her sister Louise, my brother Jonathan and his wife Yvonne – all of us numbed by the news, paralysed into inactivity by not knowing how to react. It was like a scenario for a holiday as written by Jean-Paul Sartre. We would all sit around the table in my sister's garden, not knowing what to do, or what to say, fuelled by endless cups of tea, pushed together but not united by grief, talking about everything but the elephant in the room (or on the lawn) – Lizzie's death. Just mentioning Lizzie's name reduced her father to tears, much to the annoyance of her mother and the Howe's collective and stiff upper-lipped English embarrassment. It was important to be together, but once we were together what was there to be done or said?

Time stood still.

And so, not really knowing what to do with, or for, the children, I decided we would go to the seaside as promised. And their cousins, Jennifer and Katherine, wanted to come too – which left no room in the car for any grownups apart from me.

So the five of us set out for a grand day out in Great Yarmouth.

Apart from the drive from Sudbury, I hadn't driven since I heard the news. I was scared – as if the world was waiting round the corner to ambush me, as if people would stop in the street and stare at me. I felt hideously vulnerable.

I discovered that if you keep moving you don't get depressed. So we kept moving – a picnic lunch on the beach, a walk along the promenade, ice creams with chocolate flakes ('Really, Daddy, with a flake?' 'Yes, really, Lucy.' 'Wowwww!!!! Thank you, Daddy.'), twenty-five pee each for the slot machines, and then a visit to the fun fair – which is where I came to grief.

The girls wanted to go on the Big Wheel – only it wasn't a very big Big Wheel, because it was for children only. I just couldn't squeeze inside the little gondola with the four girls, even though I tried very hard.

I stepped away, not so much embarrassed as fraught, when the guy operating it joked that I might not be under ten. I had to wait and wave at the girls while they went round and round and had a great time. I felt so alone, a solitary middle-aged man lost in a children's fun fair. I couldn't wait for the ride to finish so I could grasp Jessica and Lucy by the hand. I was so anxious that being separated from them was physically painful.

To my two girls' astonishment and their cousins' delight, I then suggested that instead of slogging back along the front to the car, we would take a pony and trap. Sod the fact that it was a rip-off and that Lizzie and I would have run a mile from such an extravagance: it was a real treat to round off a day of treats. They loved it.

The reception committee that greeted us on our return to my sister's couldn't have been more welcoming or surprised that we were all back in one piece than if we had been Scott returning from the South Pole after a hundred years away. And, mostly, we had had a wonderful day out, during which we had forgotten our troubles and just had fun.

Early that evening the phone rang.

'Jeremy, it's for you. It's the police.'

My heart was racing when I picked up the receiver. What did they want?

'Mr Howe. It's the Detective Superintendent looking after the case of your late wife.'

'Yes?'

Did they want to search our house in Oxford? Did they want to question me again? Did they still see me as a suspect, even though Robin Pask had been charged with Lizzie's death in court the day before?

'Mr Howe, my commanding officer has given the all-clear for you to go ahead with your late wife's funeral.'

'Oh, I see. Thank you.'

'Mr Howe, were you thinking of a burial or a cremation?'

'Er . . . ?'

'We would like you to bury her.'

'I see. Why?'

'In case we need to exhume her body at some point. On behalf of the North Yorkshire Constabulary, I would like to give you and your family our very best wishes. Good day to you, Mr Howe.'

'Thank you. Goodbye.'

'Oh, and Mr Howe . . .'

'Yes?'

'We would advise you to make it a low-key affair.'

'Why?'

'There'll be a lot of press interest and that will attract all sorts of weird people, you know, the kind of people who might stalk you and cause a fuss. Keep it low-key is my advice, Mr Howe.'

I was too dazed to do very much, and was more than happy for Lizzie's parents to arrange the funeral. We agreed that Lizzie should be buried in Bath, the only place that she could have called home in our rootless lives, in the same plot as her aunt, who had died the year Lucy was born. Her parents said they would pay for it all. They took the police word as gospel and wanted it to be a private cere-mony, family only. I disagreed – I wanted our friends to be there too. Maka conceded, but she had another anxiety.

'Who will look after the children?'

'I had assumed that I would. They'll come with me.'

'They can't come, surely. They're too little. They would find it too upsetting.'

I was in a state of complete confusion for the ten days leading up to the service. My instinct was that Lucy and Jessica were inseparable from me and that of course they should accompany me to the funeral. The thought of being apart from them, even for a minute, overwhelmed me. Of course, it would be upsetting for them, but weren't they upset anyway? Surely they should come?

I sought advice. Or rather, my sister sought advice, the day after the police had called me. By some miracle, she managed to get me an appointment with the head of the Children's Psychiatry Department in Norwich (waiting time approximately six months) *later that same morning*.

As I sat in the waiting room with Philippa, I felt like a fraud. I had never met a psychiatrist before. Surely all I had to do was ask the doctor, 'Do I take the children to their mother's funeral?' She would then answer yes or no, and I would go home. I could have done it by phone.

My sister and I were with her for over an hour. Although she knew my story (she too had read the papers), she wanted me to tell it in my own words. She spoke quietly and monotonously as we sat in her cool, darkened room. Time stopped. I had the space to breathe, to relax, to reason. We hardly touched on the subject of the funeral – she certainly never asked me a direct question about my dilemma – but when I left a) I wanted to hug her and b) I was beginning to know my own mind.

I had, it seems, discovered the first law of coping: trust your instincts. Don't let the heart rule your head, go lower down. Trust your gut.

By the end of the day, without ever really seeming to address the problem (actually I felt a bit cheated when it was time to go – not only had she given me no answers, she had barely allowed me to ask the question), the answer was clear.

Of course the children should come to the funeral.

If this wasn't miracle-working, I don't know what is.

'Oh, and Jeremy,' she said as we shook hands, 'if you need any more help, I know a colleague in Oxford. I will write to her and your GP and let them know you are coming.'

She was as good as her word. But that is another story.

7

Lizzie's funeral took place on a typical August afternoon – wet, blustery and grey – about a fortnight after her death.

We left Norfolk, briefly touched base in Oxford to pick up clean clothes, and moved on to Bath.

The one thing I had to do before we went was to collect my alibi – poor Milly Molly Mandy – from the cattery. I dumped the children with Julia across the road – she was Lizzie's best friend in Oxford – and raced off to pick up our hapless kitten, lodged thirty miles away. It was the first time I had really been by myself since my walk across the water meadows in Sudbury. Stuck in Oxford's appalling traffic I felt OK – well, kind of OK – but once I hit the dual carriageway I felt bereft. Each corner, each turning, each signpost on the familiar Oxford to Bath road seemed to trigger a memory of Lizzie. I felt utterly terrible – I started to weep, I started shouting Lizzie's name, I turned on the radio really loud to keep me company, but found myself shouting over the noise of the music. I drove faster and faster. I felt miserable beyond words, helpless, hopeless, sobbing. I was driving so fast that I realized I was in danger of losing control. Did I care? Of course I bloody cared!

I got a grip, slowed down, and pulled into a layby. I sat there hunched, banging my head against the steering wheel. 'Oh, Lizzie, Lizzie, Lizzie, Lizzie. I cannot, CANNOT bear it.'

I took off my glasses because they were so fogged up I couldn't see.

'Pull yourself together,' I muttered to myself. I got out of the car, walked down the road for a hundred yards, taking deep breaths, got back in, started the car and began to drive sanely.

The lady at the cattery was very understanding: she knew about what had happened because the police in York had phoned her. The cat, however, was not the least bit pleased to see me and howled all the way home as if I were her kidnapper. I was too embarrassed to behave badly in front of her, so I drove back carefully and quietly.

We got home, where she was nearly squeezed to death by the girls, I arranged for a neighbour to feed her, and then we packed up and went off to Bath, leaving Milly Molly Mandy to guard the house.

We arrived at the house where Lizzie had grown up and where we were married – her parents' home, on the western edge of the city. It was a large, honey-coloured Regency villa, which the girls treated as a second home. It had a toilet for every day of the week, and a tap for every week of the year. From the front, it looked like the kind of house a child would draw, with a beautiful magnolia tree in front, a vine-covered verandah, a large front door dead centre at the top of stone steps and big windows like eyes.

Getting ready for the funeral reminded me so much of our wedding day, only someone was missing – Lizzie wasn't there to worry about the time and get into a strop because there wasn't enough hot water for her to wash her hair. And, like our wedding, I had almost nothing to do with planning it: Maka had organized everything and my best man – my brother Jonathan – had invited people, if that is the right word to use for a funeral.

Choosing the hymns (I asked her best friend from school, who lived in America and couldn't come over, to choose ones Lizzie would have liked) and the readings, seeing the priest, whom I had never met before, looking after the children, waiting for all the relatives to arrive: it all went by in a blur. And as the clock crawled towards two o'clock, the knot in my stomach tightened.

The morning was one of bathing and hair-washing and brushing, ironing and laying out our clothes in readiness. I was brutally aware that the day's purpose was so grim that I could not really believe it was happening to me. I was caught in some horrible dream. I had arranged to go to the church with the children to see the coffin. I didn't want it to be a shock when they arrived at the service and saw the box with their mother inside for the first time. And this way we had a completely private moment to say goodbye to their Mummy.

Jessica and Lucy – helped by Julia while I was on my kitten rescue trip – had each decorated a plate with sea shells, which we were going to place on the coffin with a posy of garden flowers the girls had picked with Maka. Bearing our plates and posies, we crept into the empty church, the rain rattling on the roof tiles. Laid out on a trestle at the head of the nave was the coffin. Seeing it for the first time was heart-stopping. The girls were both excited and curious rather than daunted, and wanted to be lifted up to inspect their Mummy's coffin.

'I didn't know Mummy's middle name was Mary, like mine,' piped up Jessica, peering at the brass name plaque which read: 'Elizabeth Mary Howe 1958–1992.'

'Daddy, can I have a look too?' Lucy lifted her arms impatiently and I picked her up by the waist. 'Mummy never had a middle name!' That Lizzie had never been given a middle name had been a bone of contention with her. That Jessica had been saddled with Mary (in memory of my grandmother, who had died long before she was born) was a bone of contention with *her* – 'Mary's a horrible name' – whereas Lucy was incredibly proud of her middle name, Elizabeth.

I felt physically sick – why had I let someone else organize things and screw them up? But, for the girls, it changed the mood. They squawked and chided. 'How come the funeral people don't know Mummy's name?'

'Maybe it's not Mummy in there. Maybe she's not really dead.'

'Don't be a silly, Luce.' But I could see that Jessica wanted with all her heart what Lucy had just said to be true.

'I am afraid she is dead, my sweet,' I told her. 'It is definitely Mummy in the coffin.'

'Can we have a look, Daddy, just to make sure?'

'No, darling, you can't. It is screwed down ready for the funeral.'

'Please. I want to look at Mummy.'

'No, Lucy my sweet. I am afraid you can't. I'm sorry.'

'Daddy hasn't got a screwdriver, silly!'

'He could get one.'

On the advice of the police, the undertakers and just about everybody, the coffin had been nailed down fast. Lizzie's injuries were too horrible to witness (which was why the Assistant Coroner wouldn't let me touch the sheets when I had to identify her body), and so I am the only one of the family who saw poor Lizzie's dead body.

'I guess Maka just made a mistake,' I said.

'She does keep calling me Lizzie all the time, Daddy.'

'Do you mind that Jessica?'

'No. Not really. It's quite funny.'

For the rest of her life, Maka invariably called Jessica Lizzie. The poor woman never noticed.

I lifted each girl in turn and they very carefully placed their plates and their flowers on the coffin.

I said a simple prayer – 'Dear Lord, please look after our Mummy. Please let her know that we love her, now and always. For Jesus Christ's sake. Amen.'

The girls quietly said, 'Amen,' and then I took them by

the hand and led them out of the church. At the door, we took one last look at Mummy and then scuttled through the soaking-wet churchyard to the car and back home.

Maka was genuinely surprised about the error and got on the phone to the undertakers immediately. She really had thought that Lizzie's middle name was Mary. I realized that, beneath her brusque, no-nonsense exterior, she had lost it. I don't think she ever re-found it.

After a desultory early lunch, every mouthful of which stuck in my throat and which was eaten while the caterers for the wake took over the kitchen and clucked and cooed over Jessica and Lucy, we got ready. I could not decide what to wear – my bright tie or my black one (I only had two). Making the right choice seemed so important at the time; I swapped them round about a hundred times. And then suddenly the funeral director arrived and, almost caught unawares, we were whisked off to the church in the pouring rain.

We arrived and assembled under umbrellas, Lucy, Jessica and I at the front. It was like waiting in the wings of a theatre. The undertaker peeked into the church and then signalled to me that we were ready to enter. He pushed open the heavy door with a clatter and, to the sound of the organ, we all processed into the church.

I don't know what I was expecting, but as we entered, Jessica and Lucy tightly clutching a hand each, several hundred faces in an absolutely packed church turned round to look at us. I was buoyed up on a sea of love, hugely relieved.

As we walked up the aisle, our child minder, Catherine Unia, rushed out from her pew and thrust a bunch of flowers at Jessica and Lucy. 'For your Mummy,' she whispered breathlessly, her face flushed with emotion.

'Daddy,' Jessica whispered, 'are we sitting at the front because we're special?' She made it sound like a treat, like going with me to the theatre.

We sat by the coffin. As I ushered the girls into the front pew, I noticed that 'Mary' had been crudely excised from the brass plaque and the pretty little plates and the girls' posies had been fixed to the lid, making it look faintly like a table laid for dinner.

I couldn't believe that Lizzie was inside. I don't suppose that anyone at any funeral down the thousands of years of funerals can believe it is their beloved in that box. Death and disbelief travel hand in hand.

'Why is everybody looking at us, Daddy?' said Lucy loudly. It broke the ice. Some people laughed, some began to sob.

The service went by in a daze. I was preoccupied with helping Lucy draw a picture.

My boss read from Milton's 'Lycidas', Lizzie's favourite poem (certainly not mine, but it felt appropriate), Inga-Stina Ewbank read from Ecclesiastes, another friend from Wordsworth's 'There Was a Boy', a poem that meant a lot to me. The priest – who had only met me the day before – gave a beautiful address, we sang Lizzie's favourite hymns and said prayers. And then it was all over. So fast.

Jessica, Lucy and I filed out first behind the coffin and then, like at a wedding, we shook hands with the entire congregation. It was a very strange meet and greet, but it felt right. I don't think I'd ever been hugged by so many people in my life, but each hug restored just a little piece of the love I had had ripped away from me.

Two mourners stood out. One was a friend whose marriage had collapsed, prompting her to retrain. Lizzie – ever the teacher – had been incredibly helpful in getting her through her law exams. As she hugged me, red-eyed and red-faced with emotion, broken by grief, she said how wonderful Lizzie had been and that she would be in touch. I have never heard from her since. The other was Lizzie's tutor from Oxford. Lizzie had just applied for a lectureship at her old college and had failed even to be shortlisted for an interview. This woman had drawn up the shortlist. She could not look me in the eye.

Then came the committal at the grave. The rain had stopped and the sun was breaking out. I had compromised with Maka and Deda, and the committal was to be private, immediate family only. Not even the girls were to be there; I had arranged for my mother and sister to look after Jessica and Lucy back at the house. I had promised them that I would put some flowers from Jessica and from Lucy a fresh fig picked in Maka and Deda's garden – the fruit

Lizzie loved above all others – into the grave for them. But it was as if I were umbilically attached to them, and there was no way that we were going to go our separate ways. Nor was I going to stop all those wonderful people attending the actual burial, which took place in a cemetery at the other side of Bath, high on a hill that seemed to overlook the rest of the world.

All I can recall is streams of people hurrying over the downs towards the grave, which was surrounded with more flowers than I have ever seen in my life.

As the coffin was lowered into the grave, Jessica threw in her flowers and Lucy was about to throw in her fig, but instead tried to jump in herself.

'I want my Mummy,' she wailed. 'I want to be with my Mummy.' And, sobbing, she was scooped up by my mother.

And so Lizzie, my heart's best treasure, was buried at the age of thirty-four.

The day after the funeral, I took the girls to see the Walt Disney film, *Peter Pan*. I held Jessica's hand most of the way through, as she and Lucy stuffed their faces with popcorn (which I bought as a special treat. I mean, why not just spoil them, me, us for the rest of our lives? What was the point of holding back anymore?). Once the popcorn was finished, Lucy clambered onto my lap. My abiding image of Lucy as a toddler was of a young child sitting on her mother's lap. That's what she did. So now she did it to me.

Peter Pan is a mother-fixated story. When Peter sat on Wendy's lap and asked her to be his mother I had tears streaming down my face. I had forgotten how much the film worshipped at the shrine of motherhood, just how unsuitable it was for two girls who had just buried their own mother. 'What are you thinking, Lucy?' I asked a rapt child. I wondered if she was in a state of trauma and needed to leave the cinema.

'I was thinking what a beautiful dress Wendy is wearing.'

8

Our return to normality was prompted by Katie's birthday party.

Katie, a quiet mouse of a girl, was inexplicably Jessica's best friend.

I was so anxious about going home. Jessica, Lucy and I had to start a new life. All the rules of the game had changed, and I felt hopelessly ill-equipped to live it, but it had to happen, so off we went.

We arrived back in Oxford before lunch on a Saturday. Our new kitchen had been completed in our absence. There on the new worktops were two Disney *Little Mermaid* beakers, with a note: 'To Jessica and Lucy. I hope you enjoy your new kitchen. Love Paul.' He was our builder. There were cut flowers in every vase – my personnel officer at work had somehow got hold of Catherine, our child minder, and asked her to decorate the kitchen with flowers. I was incredibly touched. But the house was empty and quiet. It didn't feel like our home.

While the girls got changed for the party, I went looking for something.

I was looking for Lizzie.

My mother had said that she could feel my father's presence in their house in Sudbury long after his death. I searched for Lizzie everywhere, but there was nothing. She had vanished utterly. There was just silence and emptiness. No lingering smell of her in her bathrobe hanging by the shower, no imprint of her in our bed, no surprising notes or reminders left on her desk, no secret stash of love letters. Just a lot of freshly washed unneeded clothes and neat files of paperwork, her everyday objects devoid of their purpose because she was just not there to use them – her nightie under the pillow, her toothbrush in its mug by the sink, her cleansing lotion by the bed, her diaphragm (the bane of our sex life) neatly stowed in the bedside table, her lists of things to do on her return from York pinned on the noticeboard in her study, her neatly arranged papers, her wardrobe, her books. But not Lizzie. Everything was exactly as she had left it, but there was no trace of her, the person. I could not find her. There was no ghost of Lizzie. I felt cheated. With increasing anxiety, I ransacked everything, as if I was hunting for a lost wallet or key, pulled open drawers, opened jewellery boxes, smelt her clothes, riffled through her papers. Where was she? I'd been certain that I would find her once we got home – the idea of it had softened the awful prospect of coming back. But no – she had bloody well vanished.

I remembered a car that we had passed on the way from Bath: a crumpled wreck left on a verge, the bonnet wrenched open, leaving the radiator like a toothless grin, the windscreen frosted by some awful impact, the roof crumpled where it had rolled over, the sides stoved in. Smashed to bits. Lizzie's death was that car crash. I saw Jessica, Lucy and me as survivors, me standing with my arms round them on the side of the road, forlorn, stunned, but alive. All our worldly belongings scattered around us, blowing in the wind.

I was reminded of the Wittenham Clumps, where we used to picnic. Two trees on a hilltop grow around each other to form a clump – one facing the sunrise, one the sunset, each guarding their partner from the wind and the rain and the sun. Partners for life – like Lizzie and me. But what happens when one tree dies? When it is ripped out of the earth? Two trees, now one, alone and defenceless, facing the wrong way. Next to it is a gaping hole. A huge crater.

I was standing next to that hole. I was scared that we would be sucked into it and drown in grief—

'Daddy, Jessica wants to know where you put Katie's present,' Lucy interrupted my reverie. 'Why have you thrown all Mummy's jumpers on the floor, Daddy?'

'I was looking for something. Lucy, you look lovely, darling. Is that the dress Maka gave you for your birthday?' It was her only dress. Lucy didn't do dresses – 'When I grow up I want to be a boy.'

'The present's downstairs. Don't you remember, Cousin Jennifer wrapped it for us in the pretty paper with elephants on?'

'Daddy!' Jessica called up. 'I can't find my hairbrush. And we need to go or we'll be late!'

I suddenly realized that, in the girls' eyes, I was now their mummy as well as their daddy. Presents and hairbrushes and going to parties were what mummies did. As a dad, I saw myself as the Minister of Fun – 'Let's go to the fair!', 'Shall we go to the seaside today?', 'Oh, go on, buy them an ice lolly.' Lizzie was the Minister of Work – 'Eat that last carrot stick!', 'Time for bed girls!', 'Jessica, go and wash those filthy hands. Right now. Off you go!' In gaining a new mother, I wondered if they had lost their father, because I wasn't much good at being fun anymore. And I was certainly a different type of mother, mostly because a) I was a man, b) I was a working mum and c) I was inept. Whenever Lizzie had gone away – which was infrequently – I had played at being mum and had been interestingly different from their real Mummy, but, let's be honest, not much good. This was now for real, and was for ever.

'Come on, girls. Here's the present. I don't think we need coats, do you? Have you written the card, Jessica?'

'We were going to make one, remember, Daddy?'

'Oh.'

'Shall we do one now?'

'No, darling. Katie will have to go without a card or we will be terribly late.'

'But she's my best friend.'

'Honestly, sweetie, she'll understand. We've just driven two hours to get here. It'll be OK. Honestly.'

'OK.'

'Come on.'

Off we set. As I was about to slam shut the front door—

'Daddy, have you remembered the door key?'

'Shit.'

'Daddy!'

'Oops. Poo, I mean.'

They giggled.

'Lucky you reminded me.' For the next two years, practically everyone on our street had a door key to number ten, just in case I forgot.

Off we trooped across the park, me feeling as if I were walking naked and being watched by everyone. It was as if I had lost several layers of skin. We reached the door of the church hall, wide open. It was dark and it took all my courage to go inside. I stopped and gave them both a cuddle – I could see they were both as anxious as I was.

'Have fun, my sweets.'

'Aren't you coming in with us, Daddy?'

'No, I'm . . . OK. Just for a few minutes.'

What happened next was odd. Surreal. All the mums – almost none of whom I knew or recognized – were standing around talking, and all the children were clustered around Katie as she opened her presents. When we went in, everyone went quiet. It was as if ghosts had entered the room. Jessica, Lucy and I stood there, stranded.

Katie broke the silence by coming up to Jessica and

giving her a hug. And then she hugged Lucy and smiled at me.

'I am so glad you could come,' her mother whispered to me. 'Katie was so worried that Jessica wouldn't make it.'

'Don't worry, Jessica wouldn't have missed Katie's party for the world. She's been nagging me about it all week.'

'We are so sorry about your news.'

'Yes, it's awful. I can't believe it has happened. Well, yes, I can, but you know what I mean.'

'I know.' She wasn't a woman of many words, of any words actually. We stood in silence, then she asked, 'You don't know any party games do you?'

'Er . . .'

'It's just that Dave was going to do that bit, but he's had to go to work.'

Ah, I thought, one smart dad.

And so, for the next hour, I organized party games – rather manically – which mostly involved girls running around and screaming, with a bit of musical chairs thrown in. All the mothers drifted off back to their Saturday afternoons. I had nowhere to drift off to, so playing games was probably good therapy. But of this I was assured – our little community of South Oxford was in shock.

9

Katie's party had, of course, been on a Saturday. The following Monday, in rather unconventional circumstances, I began an unscheduled maternity leave. It would last the duration of the girls' summer holiday, and my job, which had been such an important part of my life, was instantly displaced while I learnt to be a mother. Well, kind of learnt.

Anger is the fourth phase of grief, so I don't need to tell you what my reaction was when the washing machine flooded the utility room upstairs. I think it had heard me promise Lizzie a couple of months before that the next time it went wrong we would get rid of it, and it clearly couldn't face the prospect of the new regime. Between us, Jessica, Lucy and I mopped the floor, washed everything by hand – otherwise we would have had an underwear crisis – and trooped off to buy a new one. It's only money, after all.

Late one morning, we heard a terrified mewing outside from Milly Molly Mandy. We all rushed out into the garden, and there she was, stuck on the roof up by the attic-bedroom window. As it was my fault – domestic goddess that I was, I should not have left the window open; Lizzie certainly wouldn't have done so – and because I owed the cat one for being my alibi, I decided to rescue her. I don't know who was more terrified, the hapless cat, the children down below or me, risking life, limb and dignity, as I half-clambered out of the window to grab her.

I got letters of condolence and support from work – people like the head of radio, the Director General and his deputy (John Birt – heard of him?). Blimey, I thought, I'm famous. For all the wrong reasons. And, every so often, my boss phoned me to see how I was getting on. Or rather, to tell me not to come into work.

Personnel phoned me to reassure me that there was no expectation of my returning to the office before I was ready. This shadowy bit of the BBC, in charge of hiring, firing and other dark deeds, reached out to me and became first a security blanket and then a friend. It was they who had arranged for flowers to be in the house on my return from the funeral, and now they sorted out how I should gradually return to work. In fact, 'they' was one woman, Kate Poulton. She was amazing, but behind her I could see the paternal hand of my boss.

My secretary was dispatched to Oxford to see if she could help sort out all the bits of my work that had been left hanging. She was lovely, but, like a lot of people, I think she was so overwhelmed by witnessing the awful-ness of what we were going through first-hand that she never ventured back into our chaos. And all the questions she asked me about work were met with a blank look of incomprehension. My overloaded brain had just deleted the answers.

One day two colleagues descended on me and spoilt me rotten. They were like ministering angels. The rain put paid to their plan to take me out for a picnic, so instead we sat around the kitchen table, which heaved under the heaps of M&S finger food they had brought with them, and we chewed the fat. They came unannounced (having checked first that I would be there) and left just as unceremoniously late on in the afternoon. It was an act of simple human warmth. I felt connected, as if I had had a holiday that afternoon.

A week later, I took delivery of a pile of boxes from the BBC – a fax machine, a modem, a printer, an answerphone, etc. I was given a complete home-working kit, with a note that read: 'Hope this helps. Clive.' My closest colleague at work had seen to it that, if I chose, I need never come to the office.

Which was great. For now. But it still left me with a Massive Dilemma.

Massive Dilemma, Part One: how could I go on with my job? I was an executive for the BBC, I worked hard and put in long hours for my living, I lived in Oxford and worked in London, etc., etc.

Massive Dilemma, Part Two: my domestic accounts.

July 1992:

my income

+ Lizzie's income
– the cost of bringing up two children
– paying a mortgage
– a small amount of childcare
= break even.

We were staying afloat; just.

August 1992:

my income
~~Lizzie's income~~
– the cost of bringing up two children
– paying a mortgage
– shed loads of childcare
= oh shit.

What was the answer?

I could have given up my job. I thought about it a lot, but I rather enjoyed my work. It also helped me know who I was, gave me an identity. I worked with some great people too – they were my friends (see above) and it paid me a decent wage. Giving up my job was actually never a serious option. I would cease to be who I was, and I was perilously close to that point anyway.

Perhaps I should move closer to work? But how on

earth could I move to London? I didn't have any network of support there. I would sink.

Should I look for a job in Oxford? Doing what?! All I really knew about was broadcasting. Unfortunately, the university didn't even have a media studies department, so that was a non-starter.

Deda tried to persuade me to live with them in Bath. The girls treated Bath as a second home and my in-laws wanted to furnish their basement for me so that I could use it as my pad and the girls could live with them upstairs. It was a very generous offer – except that their basement was as dingy as hell, all but windowless and 110 miles from my office. If I was to ever see the girls, and be a parent to them, this was clearly not an option. Just thinking about it made me think of being in prison, a kind of lodger in the basement, incarcerated in a world of single-man hell, while my family scampered around above me. Like being in a Borrowers movie directed by Roman Polanski. I shuddered.

I know that what Maka and Deda really wanted to do was to scoop up Jessica and Lucy and bring them up as their own children. Who can blame them? They had a workaholic son-in-law who showed no discernible signs of being able to bring up anything, let alone their precious daughter's precious charges. They desperately wanted to cuddle up to their bereft granddaughters, and they fully expected me to find another partner and go off into the sunset. In fact, Deda hinted at this several times.

It didn't happen. I chose to bring up the children, for good or for ill, and to remain in Oxford in the house we called home.

So I needed childcare. Tons of it. We had had a child minder, who looked after the girls for about five hours a week. Catherine was fabulous, but I calculated that I needed someone who could take them to school, pick them up from school and look after them until I got back home, and that was without thinking about the holidays. That was . . . *sixty hours a week*, starting at breakfast time, finishing at bedtime. She would need to live in. It would cost a bomb, but what could I do? I needed a nanny – a word that had never entered Lizzie's or my vocabularies.

I went to a nanny agency – something I barely knew existed until then, but about which I soon became an expert. The agency was based in a poky little office stuffed with piles of papers, up some grim back stairs behind a cinema in central Oxford. There seemed to be young women of indeterminate nationality hanging around on the landing, and it was staffed by two thirty-something women who were too busy to take much notice of me, despite my having an appointment. Eventually, I was permitted to explain what I was looking for and why.

'Ah, you see, you are a single parent and a man. We would never find a nanny who would live in with a single-parent father.'

'But . . .'

'I'm afraid I really don't think we can help you.'

'But . . .'

I doubted that I could afford whatever they were offering anyway, so I hastily came up with a Plan B: if I abandoned the idea of the nanny taking them to school, so she would start at three in the afternoon rather than eight in the morning, sixty hours miraculously shrank to twenty-five. Much cheaper! I put an advert in the local paper. But how in God's name would I make it work? How would I manage the early morning school run? After all, people might just notice if I never got to the office before eleven in the morning. But I was desperate.

With the ad in the paper I decided to at least try the other city-centre agency – just for luck. They were a lot posher and a lot more expensive. Their office was welcoming and relaxing, more like a sitting room than a place of work. The lady who ran it – a mother of three, about my age, I guessed – had a cup of tea waiting for me when I arrived, and she was incredibly sympathetic: she knew my story and she wanted to help me find a way out of my impasse. Her view was that if you can throw money at it, any logistical problem of childcare can be solved. She suggested that I see what came of the newspaper ad. If it worked, great; if not, come back to her. There was a way out of this mess! As I drove back home I felt elated.

I passed a cyclist coming in the opposite direction. Lizzie cycled everywhere, always in a hurry, always looking as if she was struggling against time. And, for one breathtaking moment, I thought it *was* Lizzie!

'Lizzie, it's going to be OK,' I said under my breath, and then louder. And again.

My heart raced. I stopped the car. I wanted to tell her that I thought it was going to be alright, that I loved her, that the girls were fine, that I was missing her like mad, that, well, Lizzie, you can come home now. But the girl on the bike rode past and she wasn't the least bit like Lizzie and I felt cheated. Bitterly disappointed. I drove on, heading back home.

But for days afterwards I felt as if I had been so close to Lizzie that I had touched her.

That, of course, would have been the solution to my problem. Have Lizzie back. I needed a wife and a mother. And a lover. What an elegant and simple solution men have come up with. But break the model and you're stuffed.

I was feeling kind of stuffed.

Of course, Jessica also had a childcare plan: 'Daddy, why don't we go round to Jane's for tea?'

'Why, darling?'

''Cos I like playing with Clara.'

Clara was Jane's daughter, a couple of years older than Jessica.

'Yes. That's a nice idea. We should do it sometime.'

'And, Daddy, didn't Clara's dad die?'

'I know, darling. How sad. She must be very sad.'

'And Jane must be sad. I'm sure she would like to see us.'

'But that was years ago, darling. Before we moved to Oxford.'

'But she must be lonely. Like you, Daddy.'

Jane lived a few doors down, with her two girls and a boy. Her husband had died about five years ago, and she – like me – was a single parent. From where I sat, her life looked like chaos. Much like ours. We duly went for tea. I liked Jane. She was feisty and fun, and surviving just fine. Unlike me.

'Why hasn't Jane got married again, Daddy?'

'You need to fall in love with somebody before you get married.'

'Like you loved Mummy?'

'Yes, darling. And I guess Jane just hasn't fallen in love.'

'Why don't you marry her, Daddy?'

'Because . . .' You could see the sense in her argument – it had a remorseless logic to it. Jane is single and a mum. Daddy is single and a dad. Ergo, they should get married and we can be one big happy family.

Onwards.

Or rather, back to the nanny. People had rung about the ad. But of course they could be anybody. I would have to check them out.

My sister Philippa helped me. We had a whole afternoon's worth of people to meet, we tidied the house, we even had a plan – we would do the introductions and then the girls would take them up to show them their bedroom. After about ten or fifteen minutes, I would go up and fetch the prospective nanny down so we could 'have a chat'. We were organized. It all felt vaguely professional.

A succession of six young women came to visit, the flotsam and jetsam of the education system, with a smattering of A levels and a succession of not very distinguished, half-hearted attempts at a career, the ones whose CVs looked promising – i.e. didn't immediately suggest alcohol dependency or certified insanity – and who had some experience of looking after children. They were all smartly turned out. All English. I had explained our predicament to them beforehand and, not surprisingly, we had a few cancellations. I wonder what on earth they expected to find once I opened our front door.

It was an exhausting afternoon, but the task was enormously simplified by Lucy.

There was only one girl to whom Lucy didn't rush up and hit, saying, 'I don't want you. I want my Mummy back.' In retrospect, it may have been because by the time she saw Linda, Lucy was tired. But I gave Linda the job.

She was to start the week the girls went back to school. The arrangement I had brokered was that I would drop the girls off at Catherine Unia's before school and either Linda or Catherine would pick them up each afternoon from school. It meant that I could go back to work. Bit by bit, I was rebuilding the edifice that had been Family Howe.

10

The rest of that summer was, well, just pretty odd.

It rained nearly every day.

I found leaving Oxford almost impossible. But I hated being at home – not that it was recognizably my home anymore; it was just the house we lived in. I developed a kind of agoraphobia.

I also developed a furrow in my forehead, the world's deepest worry line.

One morning, my poor mother, who was staying with us to help, had a stroke. It was very minor and the hospital assured us she was fine, but it showed the strain we were all under.

But life ploughed on. People – well-wishers – trooped through the house on a regular basis, all of whom wanted to hear my story. Of course, if you have a good story – and I certainly did – you like to tell it, but recounting the story of Lizzie's death became like playing and replaying a cracked record, usually with new variations put in just to embellish it, but the record was damaging the stylus, i.e. me. A friend suggested I get a T-shirt saying, 'Read the press release.' Also, people didn't really know how to react to my story because it was so far removed from their own experiences. My story was more like reading a Patricia Highsmith novel than something that happened to one of your mates.

I was visited by friends I had not seen in an age. They would come from far and wide, drop in for about an hour, and then leave. I think they just wanted to see if I was OK, and many of them never got in touch again. Some friends.

I had visits from strangers too. One, a neighbour, just knocked on the door one Saturday.

'I just wanted to share with you that I so think you did the right thing by taking your daughters to their mother's funeral.'

'Thank you.'

'It's just that my mother died when I was six and I was not allowed to go to her funeral. I felt so shut out. It still rankles with me, you know.'

'I am so, so sorry.'

'Good luck. I really mean it. But it sounds like you are doing well.'

Another was a man in a very similar position to mine. We both wondered if we could find some common ground. He had written to me, and as he lived less than an hour's drive away, I phoned him and we arranged to meet.

His wife had been pregnant with their third child and both she and the baby had died in childbirth. He was left to bring up their two other children, both younger than Jessica and Lucy. He had upped sticks and moved to a village to live almost next door to his late wife's parents, had got enough childcare to allow him to go back to work. Now, a year later, he was all but estranged from his in-laws, who were trying to take over the care of his two children, whom he was not getting on with, and he was having an affair with the nanny. The in-laws were turning him into a pariah in the village.

However inappropriately he had behaved, I felt sorry for him. But I couldn't wait to get him out of the house. In case he infected me.

By and large, I wanted the company of visitors, was grateful not to be left alone, but at the same time, I felt that my life was public property. I desperately wanted any distraction from our situation, but no matter how tricky it was, I did need to get on with real life.

Every morning I would wake up feeling acute anxiety and depressed. I just wanted to escape back into the oblivion of sleep. Then I would hear a call from the girls. 'Daddy! Can we have our juice now, please?' I would spring into action. If it wasn't for the demands of the girls making me get up, I don't suppose I would ever have got out of bed. I'd pad downstairs, feed the cat, take the girls their juice and hear about their night ('Milly Molly Mandy slept with Luce last night and not me. She doesn't like me anymore.' 'That's because you bounce around all night, silly,' replied Lucy, triumphantly stroking a purring kitten), and then sit in our new kitchen and open the mail. It was like one long lead-up to Christmas, because I got hundreds – and I mean hundreds – of cards of condolence, from everyone I had ever known and some more besides. Which somehow made me feel wanted. I would get withdrawal symptoms if I came downstairs and there were no cards waiting for me on the doormat.

After that, and once I had got the children up and given them breakfast, the structure of my days became horribly random. I had precious little idea what to do with the long days, short of playing Frustration for three hours. Sometimes I would play against myself.

One afternoon, shortly after a lunch of peanut butter on crackerbread and carrot sticks, I was lying on the sitting-room floor reading my *Guardian*, while Lucy, curled in the crook of my leg, was busy drawing.

'Daddy, if Jesus came back from being dead, why can't Mummy?' she said as she coloured in the picture of Flounder she had drawn.

'Well, Lucy, Jesus was the son of God. It's a bit different from Mummy.'

'I see.'

She carried on scribbling.

'Daddy, Snow White came back from the dead – why can't Mummy?'

'Well, darling, in the story she swallowed a poisoned apple that got stuck in her throat and when they were carrying the coffin to her funeral the seven dwarves nearly dropped it and that jolted the apple free. She was never really dead like Mummy is.'

'I see.'

More scribbling.

'Daddy – what about the Sleeping Beauty?'

I sat up, lifted Lucy onto my lap, cuddled her and told her through my tears that her Mummy was never coming back, but that she was still alive in both our memories and also deep inside in our hearts, that half of what made up Lucy was Mummy, and she would never, ever lose that.

I still don't know if she understood, but the cuddle made her feel a bit better.

A couple of evenings later, as I was putting them to bed, Jessica piped up with a familiar question.

'Daddy, you know the bad man who killed Mummy?'

'Yes, darling.'

'Where did he hit Mummy?'

I had told the girls a half-truth – that a bad man had hit their mummy and that she had died. This clearly did not satisfy Jessica.

'How did she die?' She relentlessly used this line of questioning most days. When she saw me pause, she continued to probe. 'Daddy?'

'Yes, darling?'

'How exactly did Mummy die?' she asked as she clambered up onto the top bunk.

'Well . . .'

I decided to bite the bullet.

Somewhere, I'd read that more soldiers died in the Great War of infections caused by the filth that got into their wounds in the trenches than from the shrapnel that caused the wounds.

I saw the truth as some kind of astringent that would keep Jessica and Lucy's wounds clean, wounds caused by the loss of their Mummy.

But telling them the truth wasn't exactly easy. My uncle had died in a car crash when I was a little boy. We were told what had happened and even though I wasn't yet five years old, it was something that made a huge impression. I can still remember us three sitting in the bath when my mother told us. Driving home from the office very late one night, after a few drinks, suffering from jet lag, my uncle was driving too fast, one of the tyres was under-inflated, he momentarily lost concentration and ended wrapped round a lamp post about a mile from home. He died instantly. For some reason, his daughter, my cousin Liz, who was the same age as me, had been told a different story by her mother – that he had crashed the car, but had come home and had a heart attack in the kitchen and died in the small hours. We were told never to talk about her father's death with Liz – we surmised this was because the two versions of the story didn't match. Of course, all we wanted to do after that was speculate about my uncle's death. You can see that our version was too complicated to be made up, whereas the one told to Liz – which didn't even stack up to a four-year-old – doesn't ring true. If all this had happened at home, why hadn't Liz been woken by the arrival of an ambulance? Why was her mother up in the middle of the night to witness his heart attack? Twenty years later, Liz's mother, a heavy drinker who smoked forty cigarettes a day – died of a heart attack. Liz was distraught. Her father had died of a heart attack in his thirties, her mother of a heart attack in her late forties. What hope had she? My mother had to take her to one side and tell her the truth about how her father had died.

What purpose did that lie serve? Lies are messy, the truth is clean and simple.

Clean wounds heal, dirty wounds do not.

'I mean, if you hit someone, you don't die, do you? I hit Lucy yesterday and she's not dead.'

'Well, the bad man hit Mummy very hard.'

'But how hard? Did he have a stick?'

'Well . . .'

'Did he hit her with a knife?'

'Well . . .' And I sat down at their little table and told both Jessica and Lucy that I would tell them exactly how Mummy had died, that they were not to be frightened, that it would never happen to them, that it was a horrible, freak occurrence, but that as far as I knew, this was what had happened.

'Mummy was in her room at the college in the middle of the afternoon. I bet she was working at her desk . . .'

'Did she have a cup of coffee?'

'I expect so.'

'And some dried figs?'

'I expect so. Anyway . . .'

Telling the story of Lizzie's death was like telling them a ghastly inverted fairy story.

'Anyway, a man knocked at the door. Because she was a nice polite lady, she answered the door and I think he barged in and stabbed her with a big knife for no reason at all other than he had gone mad. He was ill and he couldn't help himself and now he is safely locked away and cannot hurt anyone ever again. Mummy died almost instantly. I don't suppose Mummy felt any pain after he had stabbed her.'

On the death certificate, one of the causes was heart failure due to shock. Those last few seconds must have been . . . well, words don't take you there. In A.S. Byatt's *Still Life*, a novel that had made a huge impression on Lizzie, the heroine is electrocuted by faulty wiring in a fridge in her kitchen. In the nanosecond between the moment of shock and her death, all that goes through her mind, quite lucidly, is: 'Who will look after the children now?' I think that is probably how Lizzie died, and why my duty of care to Jessica and Lucy has been so important, above and beyond the fact that I love them unconditionally.

But I don't think that her death was painless.

'Was there any blood, Daddy?'

'Yes, my sweet.'

I had seen her bloodstained dress and the blood splattered on my briefcase at York police station.

'How much blood, Daddy?'

'A lot, I think.'

'If this was the floor in the room where she died,' she said, putting her hand against the wall by her bed, 'did it come up to here [6 inches] or here [12 inches] or here [way above her head]?'

'I don't know, my darling. I never saw where Mummy was killed. But there isn't that much blood in you or me or in Mummy. It was like a very, very, very bad cut that wouldn't stop bleeding. And if that happens, your heart runs out of blood and you die. Like Mummy did. But it happens very fast.'

'Oh.'

Pause.

'I see.'

There was a silence. I could see by the look on Jessica's face that I had put her worries – and I think her fears about how terrible her mother's death had been – to rest. She never asked about it again, not because she couldn't, but because she didn't need to. She knew. She was satisfied.

I gathered them both up in my arms and wept, and they wept, and we lay on Lucy's bottom bunk for an age as the shadows lengthened. I felt guilty that it was way past their bedtime, but we cuddled together until they were dozing. I lifted Jessica up into her bunk, and sleepily she said, 'Goodnight, Daddy. I love you, Daddy. Thank you for being such a good Daddy,' and I tucked her up and then put little Lucy, only four and without a mother, little Lucy, who had uttered not a word during the whole episode, under her duvet and cuddled her. What does it feel like to be four and not have a mummy? I could never lock on to that awful wavelength; my mind would grind to halt, because it was such an unbearable thought. Her eyes fluttered open and she smiled at me and gave me a big hug and fell back to sleep.

I crept downstairs and howled my eyes out. I had no one to tell, no one to share it with; most of all, I wanted to share it with Lizzie. But I had told the girls the truth about what had happened to their mother. I had left their wounds clean, so that they had the best chance possible of healing strongly – and I think they have – but doing so left me wrung out.

Over the next few weeks, I gradually got used to going round to Jessica and Lucy's friends' houses and chatting with their mothers while the children played together. It was the way I became a surrogate mum, and was accepted by people as such, and chatted like mums do.

'Polly, I think I might have had a stroke or something. Like my mother. I don't seem to be able to think straight anymore.'

'Oh dear.'

'It's like I've got cotton wool between my ears. I haven't read a book for weeks, only skim the papers and all I seem to be able to do is think about what meal I need to prepare next for the children.'

'That's not a stroke, Jeremy. That's called childcare.'

'What do you mean?'

'Childcare is the next best thing to having a lobotomy. Ask any mother.'

Then, one morning that August, when I was trying (and failing) to tidy up, the phone rang.

'It's the BBC here. We were expecting you for a job interview this morning and you haven't turned up. The interview board is pretty pissed off with you, you know.'

Months ago, long before Lizzie died, I had applied for a job in television drama. I had completely forgotten.

'I am sorry, but if someone had told me about the interview, you never know, I might have turned up.'

'Oh. We sent you an email.'

'But I've been out of the office for over a month.'

'Oh.'

'What am I supposed to do?'

'Well, look, can you come for the interview after lunch?'

'I'm in Oxford and I have to look after my two girls this afternoon.'

'Oh.'

'Do you know anything about me and my situation?'

'No.'

'Well, brace yourself, because it isn't a pretty story. My wife was killed earlier in the summer, I am on compassionate leave, and I'm not really in any state for a job interview.'

Real life had burst in on the weird bubble of our Oxford lives, where the world of work, which had so dominated my life, felt as distant as the moon.

'I see. But if I can rearrange the interview for this afternoon . . .'

'Well, if I can get childcare I am happy to turn up, but I should warn you, I will be totally unprepared.'

'Even so. They do want to see you.'

'Who's they?'

'The Head of Television Drama and the Head of Television Drama Series.'

Oh, so nobody important then. They only look after about half a billion pounds' worth of programmes. 'Well, you had better tell them about my situation. Oh, and I haven't watched any television for two months.'

'Not any?'

'None.'

'Not even *EastEnders*?'

'Not even *EastEnders*. And I am not sure I could do the job anymore, even if you were to offer it to me right now.'

'Hmm, I see.' He sounded affronted. 'Well, I will talk to them and get back to you.'

'I think you need to talk to my personnel officer too.'

'OK.'

And that, so I thought, was that.

After lunch, the phone went again.

'Jeremy, it's about your interview.' His tone of voice was much more concerned, much gentler, as if I were an invalid.

'Yes.'

'I have spoken with the two heads, and they still want to see you. And I have spoken with your personnel officer. I get the picture. I am so sorry about your loss. Would three o'clock be OK for you?'

'I'm in Oxford. I can't possibly get there in time.'

'Er . . . when is good for you?'

'If I was to come, I couldn't get there much before five – unless I was to drive.'

'Shall we say four? And I will get you a parking space at TVC.'

Being offered a parking space at TVC – Television Centre – was a bit like being offered a bag of gold. They must be serious, I thought. They had fixed for me to park in the Director General's space ('He's in Edinburgh this afternoon. You will need to vacate it by seven this evening').

'If I can get childcare. But do make sure that they know about my personal circumstances, and I should reiterate, I really don't think I could do the job even if they offered it to me.'

'Of course. And I will let you know about parking in the next twenty minutes. I will talk to them about your concerns.'

Well, I had about half an hour to prepare for the job of Senior Development Executive for TV Drama Series and sort out who would look after the children while I went for the interview. A friend across the road was dead impressed. 'They must want you. Of course, I'd love to look after the girls. What will you wear?'

'I might change my shirt, if I can find a clean one.'

So my preparation for the interview consisted of ironing a shirt. I figured that somebody wanted me – and it gave me a sense of self-worth, that I wasn't just the washed-up wreckage that I felt like.

The main thing I remember about the interview was just how comfortable the chairs were and what delicious chocolate biscuits they gave me with my Earl Grey tea, served in a china cup. My interviewers were on their best behaviour, and could not have been nicer. That might have been because as I sat down, I asked them to be nice to me, otherwise I might burst into tears.

'Thank you for coming. I realize how difficult it must have been for you. We just wanted to meet you.'

We talked as much about childcare as about television, they wished me well, and then, just before I left, I said, 'Look, in the unlikely event of you offering me the job, it's almost inconceivable that I would be able to take it.'

'We understand. Of course. But thank you for coming. And good luck with everything.'

My personnel officer phoned me the next day. 'You won't want to hear this, but they were very impressed with you yesterday.'

'How come? I displayed no knowledge of television and we talked mostly about what a crap mum I was being.'

'They liked you. They think you're a crap mum who's got balls,' she laughed.

The story has a happy ending: they didn't offer me the job, but for about six weeks they couldn't decide between two candidates – me and the guy who got the job, who happened to be my best friend in the department I worked for. All I can say is, the rest of the field must have been truly shit, but it did my sense of self-worth a power of good.

Back to picking up the pieces – of which there were many. The bureaucracy of death is horrible. Read Kafka to get the gist of what you need to go through.

Before we had been allowed to bury Lizzie's body, we had to wait for the coroners' court verdict. The death certificate that was issued was horribly graphic. Requesting multiple copies of this stark document – in order to change bank accounts, house deeds, mortgages, etc. – left me reeling. The document filled me with horror each time I sent it off and opened the returned copy, and underlined what trauma Lizzie had gone through in her final moments.

Then there was child allowance, which had to be redirected. Do you know that if a husband dies, the widow gets a one-off lump sum payment and increased child support, but if the wife dies, the widower gets nothing? According to the Secretary of State for Pensions, who replied to my distraught letter on the subject, there are statistically so few single-parent fathers it just isn't worth the cost of the administrative machinery to set it up. Or at least it wasn't in 1992.

Receiving the cheque book for my newly created single as opposed to joint account hardly signalled the beginning of a joyful new life.

And so on and so on. There is no handbook that tells you what to do, no checklist, just a mess of post asking you questions that you can't answer or wish you didn't have to. I tried seeking advice – I went to a single-parent support group. But it was such a scary prospect that, having walked through the door, I walked straight out again. It felt like a dating agency to me, and I felt like an intruder. The man at the Citizens' Advice Bureau – where I had waited ages to be seen, anxiously aware that my childcare back home was running out – had no advice for me at all. He even seemed to imply that my problem was beyond their remit, that there was no citizens' advice on coping with my particular car crash of a situation.

Money was a big issue – I was spending it like water. We downsized – I got a smaller bed and a smaller car, to mirror our smaller family – but we never got smaller bills.

We were not helped by my mortgage company. One August morning, a letter landed on my doormat addressed to Mr J.P. Howe and Dr E. Howe (deceased). I was intrigued. I opened it – 'Dear Mr J.P. Howe and Dr E. Howe (deceased) . . .' This was astonishing. Someone had even had the gall to sign the letter. Did they not think it a bit strange to be writing to a dead person? But the contents of the letter were chilling – because I had not been paying my mortgage, they were taking steps to foreclose on our house. WHAT THE F**K!? I phoned my bank to check that my standing order from our (now my) account was still operating. 'Well, as far as we know, unless you have asked us to cancel them, all your direct debits and standing orders should still be working, Mr Howe. We'll check and get back to you.'

Ten minutes later they called back and said that, actually, my standing order for the mortgage had been cancelled.

'Not by me.'

'The mortgage company cancelled it.'

Bloody hellfire!

I rang the mortgage company. After an eternity, I got through to the right department – 'Mr Howe, it is company practice to cancel all mortgage repayments on the death of our clients, because most of our mortgages are insured.'

Because our mortgage was so expensive, Lizzie and I had decided to insure it on my death only, as I was the main earner.

'Cancel without informing me?'

'Yes.'

'And then threaten me with foreclosure?'

'Well, obviously that was only a warning letter. We would allow two more non-payments before we take action.'

'But without telling me that you had cancelled it?'

'That was an error on our part. Please accept our apologies.'

'And you think the best way of informing me is to write to me and Dr E. Howe (deceased)?'

'Well, obviously someone made a mistake. We would like to apologize for that too.'

'I will only accept a written apology from your Managing Director.'

'If you wish to make a complaint—'

'Too right I do.'

I am sure you get the gist of the conversation. They did apologize eventually, and so instead of them paying off my £125,000 mortgage the repayments began to drain my bank account once more. If only we had paid that little bit more to insure Lizzie's life too.

11

I had cancelled the trip to Portugal we had planned to take shortly after Lizzie's return from York, and that put the lid on a summer holiday. I was in no fit state to organize another one. But then my friend Clive insisted that I accompany him on a trip he was thinking of making to the west of Ireland.

Clive and I, both English, had met on the plane home from the BBC job interview in Belfast. We hit it off, were both offered jobs there and became firm friends.

Clive had taken a cottage in remotest Donegal for a week, while his wife, Elaine, was off in the States filming. He had care of Joe, aged ten months. His parenting skills were on a par with mine. He needed a companion, so he chose me.

Was he nuts? With me? Had he any idea what kind of a companion I would be? So I agreed.

I did the packing. I had absolutely no idea what to pack, so I packed everything the children owned. Apart from their underwear, which I left behind in our new tumble-dryer.

While I was ransacking the wardrobe to prepare for this

expedition, there was a knock at the door. I raced down-stairs and there, on the doorstep, was a familiar figure.

'Jessica, Lucy, Mr Townsend's here to see you.'

'What, Daddy? Who?' came screaming from upstairs. There was a lot of thumping and giggling.

'Mr Townsend. You know, your Headmaster.'

The thumping and giggling stopped instantly.

Mr Townsend was a sweet man, short, bearded, smiley, always pushing his specs back up his nose. He was faintly chaotic, but – in his delightfully left-wing Oxford way – ran a good school in a series of rambling workhouse-like Victorian buildings clustered around a playground, a stone's throw from the park across our street. The school was the focal point of our bit of Oxford – the centre of our little community. The one thing that mystified both Lizzie and me about Mr Townsend was that he always wore suits that didn't fit him.

'Hello, Jessica. Hello, Lucy,' he called out, considerably less bellicosely than me. 'I just popped round to see how you are.'

Two solemn-looking girls marched slowly down the stairs. They looked worried – you generally only get to speak to the Headmaster if you have done something wicked, so what on earth could they have done that merited him coming round to the house *in the middle of the summer holidays*?

Once they realized he had simply come round to say how sorry he was about Mummy, my two warmed up and we quickly settled down to play the National Trust Animal Game, which someone had just given us. It was a rubbish game that would keep a brain-dead two-year-old entertained for less than five minutes, but even with Lucy patiently and sweetly explaining the rules to Mr Townsend, he didn't really seem to grasp its subtleties. But he made instant friends of the children and they were quickly at ease, telling him where he had gone wrong with each turn in the game and their news, i.e. that they were going away on holiday and that their Mummy had died.

He had really come round to talk to me, wanting to ask how I thought we should handle the announcement of Lizzie's death to the rest of the school. It was decided that the girls would perform some 'important errand' with one of their teachers, while the announcement was made at mid-morning assembly on the first day back, and for them to slip into the hall surreptitiously afterwards with Mrs Naumann, who had been Jessica's form teacher, and whom both the girls adored. Why we decided on that, I am not sure – but it was a sure sign that the school cared.

As a special sneak preview of the coming term, he told them that Jessica was to be in Mr Standish's class, a new member of staff, while Lucy was to remain in Michelle's nursery class, where Elizabeth, her favourite teacher in the school, was the classroom assistant. I was anxious about the former (Who was he? Was he any good? How would he handle a volatile Jessica?) and relaxed about the latter, but the girls treated this as Extra Privileged Information, revelled in it and couldn't wait to rush off to tell their friends.

'I wonder if Mr Standish will be strict?' mused Jessica after her headmaster was safely out the door.

'He's a man teacher, he is bound to be strict,' cooed Lucy, as she guzzled the juice I had just given her, smug in the knowledge that Elizabeth was the Best Teacher in the Whole Wide World.

My holiday packing continued, and I got in a panic over just about everything – you know the way it is before you go away, when you feel you need to have everything neat and tidy. My major panic was what would happen to the children if the plane crashed and I died (well, if the plane crashed, they'd probably die too – but I wasn't being entirely rational). Now, you need to understand my fragile state of mind – with Lizzie's utterly random death, I felt vulnerable. If it could happen once, I reckoned, it could happen again. There was no insurance against it. I needed to make a will. A solicitor friend in London I phoned said she didn't do wills and that I should speak to someone locally. Getting nowhere fast, at five o'clock on a bank holiday Friday evening, I just typed one out on a piece of A4 paper, stating that if I were to die, I would leave everything to the children and that Philippa would have custody of them. I asked a neighbour to witness it.

'A lot of people in the street have been writing their wills since your wife died.'

I also rang the Open University: I was nursing a grudge

about their silence – the Vice Chancellor had said to the press that he had been in touch with the family to offer his condolences. Well, not to me he hadn't. What is more, Lizzie had been contracted to do a week's work and, through no fault of her own, she had been unable to do it. The university had agreed to pay all her travel expenses, but no money had been forthcoming. And I was running short of cash. I eventually got through to the summer school director, who bizarrely said that they had been trying to get in touch with me – 'Well, you could try phoning my home number, which you have on Lizzie's contact details, a copy of which I have here in front of me,' I replied tartly. He meekly offered the Open University's condolences and said he would look into the matter of the Vice Chancellor's remarks, but that he could not pay Lizzie's outstanding wages until probate was cleared.

'But there is no will and therefore there will be no probate.'

'We need proof of her death and proof of who the beneficiary is.'

'Excuse me,' I retorted, 'if you need proof of her death, just read a newspaper. It happened, in case you were unaware, while she was working for you. And, as her husband, I am her beneficiary.'

'There is no need for you to lose your temper, Mr Howe, but we do need proof.'

I lost my temper, and we parted company with me slamming down the phone and kicking the cat, which I tripped over. The bloody man even wanted receipts to cover Lizzie's train fare. 'They are with the police in York,' I snarled at him.

I wrote a careful letter to the Vice Chancellor outlining my long list of grievances and faxed it through. On our return from Ireland, there were about six messages from his office on the answerphone, a letter, a cheque and a lot of humble pie, which resulted in the establishment of an Open University trust fund in Lizzie's name.

Next morning, Lucy's godfather, Eoin, drove us to Heathrow and flew with us to Belfast, where we stayed overnight with our friend Aine and her family. Going on holiday as a threesome felt very strange, as did going back to Belfast en famille without Lizzie.

The next day Katy, Aine's eldest daughter, older enough than my two to be worshipped by Jessica, took us to the playground round the corner, where Lizzie had often taken the girls to the swings when we had lived there.

As Jessica, ever fearless, clambered up the highest of slides, Lucy followed and, suddenly becoming scared, faltered halfway up.

'Daddy, I'm stuck,' she cried. The idea had been for me to catch them at the bottom, but clearly I was now going to have to slide down with Lucy. As Jessica whizzed down towards the arms of Katy, I called, 'Back in Oxford, a slide even half this height would have rubber matting at the bottom, not concrete. What happens if Jessica falls off?'

'Belfast is a hard city,' replied the ten-year-old.

After lunch we were to set off to join Clive. I was planning our route and asked Lucy if she would stand at the front door to mind the car, as I had left it unlocked. As she opened the door of the house she called, 'Daddy, help!'

I rushed to see what the matter was. Standing at the end of the garden path was a British Army soldier, with his gun trained on our front door, in effect aimed at poor Lucy.

'Only on patrol, mate! Have a good one!'

'Cheers!' and I got Lucy, who had rushed into my arms, to wave at him.

Surveying our loaded car, Aine suggested, 'Wouldn't you prefer to stay here for the week. I'll cook you meals, we can have chats, you can go for days out and we will spoil you rotten.'

'What about Clive?'

'He's mad. He can look after himself. Stuff Clive.'

I so very nearly hoiked the children out of the car, but instead we drove off, heading westwards. It was an adventure, after all.

The car we had borrowed from friends had a sunroof. I'd never had a car with a sunroof and the girls begged me to have it open. Fine. Then it started raining (this was Northern Ireland after all) and I couldn't get it to close.

I stopped the car, but still didn't know how to operate it. So we all put our cagoules on and drove through the rain as if we were in an open-top bus.

Some miles later, there was a voice from the back. 'Daddy, I need a wee.'

'OK, darling, we'll stop as soon as we find somewhere.'

Miles later, no toilets.

'Daddy, I do need a wee.'

'I do too, Daddy. And I'm thirsty,' chorused Jessica.

This was a new experience – not the needing a wee bit, but the three of us alone in the car, with no Lizzie to turn round and minister to their needs. Eventually I got used to the front passenger seat being covered with cartons of juice and healthy snacks and tissues and maps and what have you—

'Daddy, I really do need a wee.'

Eventually we found a layby with a public toilet, where a new problem confronted me: Lucy needed to be looked after – she was only four, not all that long out of nappies and had never been to the toilet by herself in a public place. There was no way that I was going to take her to the gents' and no way I was going into the ladies' loo. What to do?

On this occasion, I just shepherded them into the ladies' and waited outside like an anxious expectant father, and of course Jessica looked after Lucy, and several ages later they came out, merry as crickets, Lucy wearing only one shoe.

'Lucy dropped her sock in the toilet, so we had to fish it out. A nice lady helped us dry it off on the hand-dryer, but it's still a bit wet.'

'Silly Billy.' Lucy just grinned at me.

I didn't ask why she was taking off her shoes and socks to go to the toilet. Some things are best left unasked.

At lunchtime the next day, we arrived in Donegal to

join Clive and baby Joe. The cottage overlooked the sea, which was grey, like the sky, and it was raining – typically Irish rain, a gentle drizzle coming in off the Atlantic. Joe had kept Clive up all night, but hey ho, off to the beach we went. Surely, no one could expect two men, a baby and two little girls to do anything sensible like unpack. Lunch was late and consisted mostly of biscuits, with a few packets of M&Ms to liven it up, and then we went shopping. For kites and jigsaw puzzles. Oh, and a packet of bacon, a tin of beans, some crackerbread, Nutella (strictly forbidden by Lizzie, but from now on the first item in the trolley on a holiday shop) and a bottle of Paddy's, of course.

Despite the weather, our stay was a great success – mostly because Jessica and Lucy took endless pleasure in mothering Joe, feeding him ('Clive, can we feed Joe tonight?' 'With pleasure'), changing his nappies ('Clive, I think Joe has done a poo. Do you want us to change the nappy for you?' 'With pleasure'), amusing him and singing him lullabies to send him to sleep while Clive and I got on with the humungous jigsaw puzzle of the world we had bought. It struck me as a brilliant arrangement.

Every so often, we would go on a jaunt. Rock-pooling, kite-flying, sandcastle-building, jumping over the freezing Atlantic breakers as they surged over our castle, ice-cream expeditions, that kind of thing. I discovered that my girls were good travellers, but no one could accuse them of being curious ones.

When I was young, as one of three children, there was a

rota for sitting by the window on car journeys and when it was my turn, I just loved sitting watching the world go by, drinking it all in as we drove. My two just listened to tapes, one earpiece per girl, or read – something I could never do, as I would get car sick. Some years later we were driving through France, the day after the latest Harry Potter book had come out (before Harry Potter, Lucy used to read the *Beano* and the Argos catalogue. Thank you, J.K. Rowling, for making Lucy a reader!), and as we whizzed through the dullness that is Champagne, I randomly called out, 'Are you alright, girls?'

'Shh, Daddy,' Jessica whispered. 'Lucy is sobbing. I think Dumbledore has just died.'

I don't think my two ever looked out of the window; they showed no interest in the world whizzing past, and sometimes continued to take no notice even after we had arrived.

'Look, darlings,' I said, having stopped the car at the top of a pass in Donegal looking down to a sweeping sandy bay, islands dotting the horizon. 'Look at that view. Isn't it beautiful?'

'I can't see it, Daddy.'

'Why not, Lucy?'

'I've got my eyes shut,' she said.

Late one afternoon I went off alone with the girls and we ended up on a narrow jetty in a harbour, with the car facing the wrong way. Clearly I needed to turn it round, but it was a bit tricky, as there were sheer drops into the sea on either side.

'If I'm not careful I'll drive off into the sea and we'll have to swim home,' I laughed nervously.

'Good,' said Lucy. 'Then we'll all drown and we can join Mummy in heaven.'

She meant it.

Perhaps the high/low point of the holiday was when we were packing to leave. We Howes could afford to be quite leisurely, but Clive had a plane to catch and was in a hurry. We were tidying up the wreckage we had created in the house (doing washing up for the first time in a week, you know the kind of thing) when Clive, being a bit vigorous with the cold-water tap, wrenched it off. Water was gushing out over the kitchen floor in a rather satisfying arc.

We panicked, as you do. While Clive tried to mop up the kitchen floor (which was a bit sandy, so it needed a wash), I searched high and low for the cold-water stopcock. No luck. We swapped places. Clive had no luck. Heads were scratched.

'Ooh, look, Lucy, there's a fountain in the kitchen,' squawked Jessica.

'Daddy, why don't you just turn off the tap?'

'Not now, Lucy. Go and play. Go on. There's a good girl.'

'We just wanted to know where to pack our dirty washing.'

'Put it in the green bag.'

'But it's full.'

'Make it fuller.'

'Daddy, water's seeping onto the living-room carpet.'

'Bloody hell!'

'Can we help mop it up?'

'Good idea.'

While the girls mopped, Clive and I decided that we needed a plumber. But where to find one? We were in the middle of nowhere, with about half a dozen empty holiday cottages and then nothing for miles. And miles. And miles. The nearest plumber was probably to be found in Boston, Massachusetts.

'I'll phone for one.' Clive, flash git, had a mobile phone. Only problem – there was no signal. Ireland didn't do mobile phones back then.

'Look, I'll drive until I find a phone box and see if I can raise a plumber.'

'I seem to remember there's a phone box at the cross-roads.'

'Where's that?'

'Er . . . about five miles from here.'

As I was unlocking the car, an elderly man in a tweed cap cycled past, on the way to nowhere, from nowhere.

'Lovely day!' he called. It was raining.

'Hi! I don't suppose you could help us? Our kitchen tap is spouting water and we need a plumber. Do you know where we can find one?'

'Which house would that be?'

'Over there.' I pointed – to a house that by now was probably more like a fish tank inside than a cottage.

'Ah, I built that house, d'you know. I'll fix it for you, no problem. No problem at all.'

So there is a God.

We entered the house, to see Jessica and Lucy ferociously mopping and Clive struggling with a bawling baby.

'That's a fine mess you've got there. I'll see if I can fix it.'

And he did. It took him a couple of minutes. We offered him money.

'Sure, I wouldn't dream of it.'

We offered him half a bottle of whisky we hadn't managed to drink.

'Well, I'll be thanking you kindly.' He put it in his jacket pocket, put his cycle clips back on, and pedalled off.

When we got back to Belfast, Aine said that she had prepared supper for us all every night because she expected us back early. There's confidence in our childcare skills.

I had survived my first holiday! I had coped, and I had had fun. Clive even said that I wasn't as miserable as he had feared. It was then that I realized what an incredibly heroic thing he had done – offering to spend a week alone with the most miserable man in the universe. And every year for the next ten years Clive and his wife Elaine took us on holiday with them – Dingle in Co. Kerry at New Year (we had a power cut on arrival and the girls and Joe shared a tepid bath by candlelight), France, Italy, Spain, Blackpool. They arranged it, we turned up. It was the best gift anyone could have given us.

12

Turning the key in the lock of the front door on our return from Donegal left me with a sinking feeling. I was walking back into reality: the silent, empty house, the unpaid bills, the unopened post, the struggle to keep going, and the cat and the children to be fed. It was the beginning of the rest of our lives, and it wasn't going to be easy. I was terrified that we might drift and sink – unless I made things happen.

In fact, once we were back, with the school holidays almost over, the pace of things changed dramatically. It was as if we had escaped from limbo, but the road ahead was uncertain, and God alone knew where it might lead. The fifth phase of grief is the rebuilding of normality.

On the last day of the holidays, Linda started. We all went out for supper to a local American diner. A family outing like this without Lizzie still felt strange, but I put myself in the waitress's shoes. To her, we must have looked like any old family, and I felt rather pleased.

Then came the new term at school.

Hand in hand, we crossed the park. Other mums with children in tow waved at us. There was that back-to-school autumnal nip in the air. We waved back, but I felt very tense. Although I used to take the girls to school from time to time, it was a rarity, with only a quick peck on the cheek at the school gate before I would be off. Now I would have to go in through the school gates myself. It was like *my* first day back, not least because I realized that I didn't really know what to do – where to leave the girls, where to hang up Lucy's hand-me-down jacket. I was only an honorary mum; I knew hardly any of the real mums. At what point should I leave and go back home? It was all new to me.

I stood at the school gates, one girl clamped to each hand. Playground life whirled around us, but no one came to talk to us, neither mothers nor children. It was as if there was an invisible chalk circle drawn around us, an unseen barrier that separated us from the rest of the world. We looked like everyone else, were breathing the same air, walking the same streets, but appearances are deceptive – we were like aliens visiting from a distant planet, the planet of grief, and deep down everyone in the playground knew it. Stretching a hand out to reach us was superhumanly difficult – I guess because no one wanted to go near the awful, devastated place we'd come from, in case we'd brought contagion with us. Only the heroic – or the similarly afflicted – could enter.

But Jessica knew what to do. She took control, showed me where they should hang their coats, showed me where Lucy's classroom was and led us to her own classroom. We walked past Mr Standish, young, tall, fresh-faced and mobbed by flirting six-year-old girls and their equally flirting mums. Jessica, busying herself with unpacking her bag, said, 'You can go now, Daddy,' half telling me, 'It's OK, you've done what all mums need to do, well done,' and half, 'Can I get on now, please, Daddy. Get lost.' As I left with Lucy, Mr Standish caught my eye and smiled at me. It made me feel less like an interloper, and this alien place teeming with unfamiliar children felt just that bit more human.

As I tripped over scampering boys in the unfamiliar corridors, I took Lucy to the nursery. I knew she knew Michelle and that Elizabeth was the Best Teacher in the Whole Wide World, but I didn't know them, was not even sure I would recognize them, but of course they knew me, because, alas, we were celebrities, and the moment we entered they both swept Lucy up. I was assured that she was indeed in safe hands.

Half of me wanted to race home and get the hell out of there, half of me wanted to dawdle, to see if I could engage in friendly conversation to kill time, but all the mums seemed to be busy, to have purpose, whereas I had none. I walked back across the park, wondering how on earth I would fill my day till three o'clock. What do mums do all day? Without the girls, I was nothing. At the tender age of four and six, my two had given me empty-nest syndrome.

It turned out that Jessica loved Mr Standish and thought he was a hoot. She thought the day when he didn't turn up 'and Mr Standish's brother taught us instead and he was really funny' (actually, they were so similar that I suspected that there was no brother and it was a hoax) was the best ever, and settled back into school quickly. It was helped by the fact that someone told her that her Mummy had met Mr Standish on the last day of the summer term and had liked him. With her mother's approval – whether or not the story was true, I had no idea – Jessica was always going to approve of Mr Standish. At the end of term parents' evening, Mr Standish told me that she was one of the most normal, well-balanced children in the class, as bright as a button and eager to learn. I came out of the meeting with a spring in my step.

I then went to see Michelle. She told a different story.

'All I can say, Mr Howe, is that Lucy got through the term. Let's say she has been treading water.'

'I see. What do you mean, treading water?'

'Well, Mr Howe, she spends most of the day sitting on Elizabeth's lap. She doesn't play with the other children, she doesn't join in. She just wants to be cuddled. I'd say she was depressed.'

I was heartbroken and angry. My poor Lucy. I felt helpless. What could I do for her to make things better?

I always understood Jessica. For all her mood swings and tantrums, she was very articulate about what had happened and very transparent in her behaviour. I was out walking with them one day along the river towpath, Jessica holding my hand, talking nineteen to the dozen, Lucy silent on my shoulders, her hands resting on my head. We were talking about Mummy.

'Do you mind talking about Mummy, darlings?'

'No, Daddy,' said Lucy.

'No. I like talking about Mummy. She was special,' and Jessica chirruped on about how sesame snaps and plain scones were Mummy's favourite food.

We talked about Mummy a lot, almost always as if she were present. We would talk about how nice she was, what a good Mummy she was, about how cross she got when they were bad girls, etc., etc. 'Mummy could be very shouty couldn't she, Daddy?' (Understatement!) 'Mummy didn't like mess did she, Daddy? You don't seem to mind mess half as much as she did.'(Oh my God, even my girls had noticed what a tip the house had become). 'Mummy wasn't a very good driver was she, Daddy?' 'No, she hated driving.' 'But she passed her test first time. Not like you, Daddy.' I never wanted to turn her into a beatified mother figure. I wanted her to be real to them.

'I do like talking about Mummy, but when we do talk about her, I don't like it so much when you get sad and begin to cry. Like you are about to now.'

Jessica was right. I could feel the tears welling up; it was like a pain barrier that I had to get through, so I soldiered on, and wept and talked. I could feel Lucy stroking my hair, Jessica gripping my hand all the more tightly. They got used to seeing their Daddy cry, but I figured it didn't matter – if their Dad had licence to cry, then so did they.

I could see that Jessica was practical and got on with things, and sometimes she tried to be the mummy in the house. 'I turned out all the lights after you because I didn't want us to waste electricity – you always get cross when the electricity bill comes, Daddy.' 'I think Lucy is running out of clean knickers, Daddy.' 'Daddy, have you packed the toothbrushes? You know you forgot them last time.' In spite of this, I tried really hard not to let her be anything other than a child – it just wasn't fair on her. I didn't want her to grow up too fast, but she was very watchful. Not long ago, she asked me why I thought that Lucy always sat behind me in the car and she on the other side – and on holidays abroad, when we hired a left-hand-drive car, why they swapped places with each other.

'Er . . .?'

'I was always worried that you drove too fast and would get arrested by the police, and I wanted to be able to see the speedometer. And when you went too fast, I would say something like, "Daddy, I feel a bit sick. Do you think you could slow down a bit, please?" But I always waited a long time before I asked you.'

'Why, sweetie?'

'Because I didn't want to make you cross.'

And she had terrible mood swings.

'Daddy, I can't decide what to do,' was always the prelude to a tantrum. Once I was standing in a playground with my friend Maddie, with whom we'd had lunch, and we were watching the girls play with her two when Jessica started behaving awfully, standing there shouting at me and blubbing about something or other. I tried comforting her, to no avail, I tried getting cross with her, to no avail, and so I just sent her packing with the stern admonishment that if she didn't pull herself together we'd go straight home, right this minute. 'That's not fair.' She stormed off in a terrible sulk and just stood in the playground looking bewildered.

'What's the matter with Jessica?'

'God knows.'

'She's in a right state.'

'I know, and I have no idea why. I can't decide if it's a normal childish tantrum or because she is upset about her Mummy. Either way, I have no idea how to cope with it, whether to shout at her or cuddle her or both.'

On the way home, driving down the motorway (i.e. when I was in no real position to bite back), with Lucy out like a light, Jessica, slightly recovered but still tetchy, and after I had refused to give her a sweet or some such, said very very quietly, 'I wish you had died and not Mummy.'

There followed a Very Long Pause while I considered my response. Then, calmly and sweetly, 'That's not a very nice thing to say, is it, darling?' And then I let her stew in it.

When we got home she gave me a huge cuddle. 'I am sorry I was nasty, Daddy. I don't know why I was so horrible. I love you, Daddy.' She was brilliant at making up. But, boy, did she have demons inside her.

She had also known how to rub Lizzie up the wrong way, almost like playing on an instrument. She has the same fiery Serb temperament as her mother, and knew how to make her really cross, the standard punishment for which was to shut her outside the back door until she cooled down. Once the girls had some friends round to play and she started, and indeed then continued, to behave so bossily, even after several yellow-card warnings, that Lizzie frogmarched her to the back door, thrust her out, and locked it behind her, exiling her to the garden. 'Bloody child.'

Seconds later, Jessica – aged four – appeared at the dining-room window, standing on tiptoe and shouting, 'Mummy, this is ridiculous.'

One Sunday evening, just before bedtime, she was in a right strop and being horrible to Lucy. I started shouting at her and put her to bed without her usual bedtime story, which showed her that I was dead cross with her. Predictably, she couldn't get to sleep. Eventually, I brought her out from the bedroom and into the hall and had a Grown-up Talk with her.

'Jessica, what exactly is wrong?'

She thought for a moment.

'Well, Daddy, you remember when Maka came last week?'

'Yes.'

'And she gave us a tube of Smarties?'

'Yes.'

'And you shared them out between Lucy and me?'

'Yes.'

'Well, Lucy got the extra one. And you promised that

the next time we got Smarties, I'd get the extra one. And when we had some yesterday, you ate the extra one.'

Do you laugh or do you cry? Well, I laughed. There was – and is – a wonderful transparency about Jessica, and deep down I knew how to handle her, probably better than Lizzie had been able to.

But Lucy?

It troubles me now that I could never get on her wavelength. Even now, whenever I try to imagine what it is like to lose your mother at the age of four, my mind very quickly hits a blank and forbidding wall.

My image of Lucy before Lizzie's death was of a little girl sitting on her mother's lap, just happy to sit there and be there. She would climb down and go off on little expeditions and forays, always knowing Mummy's lap was there to come back to, and come back she would. She never talked much, rarely lost her temper, was quick to laugh and incredibly easy to cuddle. Jessica was wiry and demanding; Lucy was sweet and very self-contained.

It is a family joke that whereas Jessica had about a million cuddly toys, each one named after either foodstuffs (the most famous being the gibbon Banana Custard – who can't be trusted because he's keen as mustard, is Banana Custard – and Strawberry, a giant strawberry) or colours (Red Ted, Blue Duck, etc. – you get the gist), Lucy only had two she really liked, and both were called Dennis.

'If you had children, what would you call them, Lucy?'

'Dennis, of course. I like the name Dennis.'

'And if it's a girl? Denise?'

'Don't be silly. That's a horrible name.'

When we talked about where Mummy was now, Jessica would say that Mummy was sitting in heaven, sunbathing on a deck chair, eating figs, drinking scalding-hot coffee and reading a detective novel. Lucy never told me about what she imagined. The only way she could articulate seemed to be through silence.

Years later, I made a drama documentary about it for Radio 4, where I interviewed a whole gang of children, including Jessica and Lucy, about what it feels like when a parent dies. The interviews were extraordinarily honest. Lucy told me that she used to like to creep up to the attic in Maka and Deda's house and look at Mummy's wedding dress and think that one day she might wear it for her own wedding. But making the programme cast no revealing new light for me on how Lucy, or any four-year-old, copes with the trauma of bereavement. I was left thinking that . . . well . . . you just get used to it, allow it to become normal, and, like the rest of us, you take each day one at a time and get through it as well as you can. But every day I could see how hard it was for her, because the enormity of her loss was incomprehensible to her.

Some years later, she made friends with a girl called Bea, whose mother had just recently died of cancer.

'Daddy, I can't decide if it's better for your mummy to die like Bea's, which was so slow and horrible, or like Mummy, which was so quick.'

'No, nor can I, darling.'

'I think it is better like the way Mummy died.'

I am not sure I agree, although of course you are left with happy memories of a fully functioning, fit mum, rather than one who was terminally ill, but that was what Lucy was used to. It had become normal in a way; it was how she accommodated loss.

In the end, I decided that the only way that I could really help her was by being the best dad I could possibly be, by making her life normal and by giving her cuddles, 'loves' as she called them. Lots of them. By letting her know I was always there for her.

Two incidents from primary school stand out.

The first was that, every morning, if I took Lucy to school, once we got to the nursery classroom, she would choose a book for me to read to her. Usually the same books – either Topsy and Tim or Janet and Allan Ahlberg's *Bye Bye Baby*. I would read it to her while she looked at the pictures, but, that apart, Lucy showed little interest in either books or reading. Then, the following year, she went up to big school (an easy transition – she went from one playground to another) and with a new classroom (next door to the old one), she had a new set of books to choose from.

'Do you want me to choose a book for you, Lucy?'

'No. I'll choose.'

I settled down with her to read.

'No. I'll read to you.'

'Er, but, Lucy, you can't read.'

'I can now I am in the Big School.'

And, word perfect, sight unseen, she read me the book. That is so typical of Lucy – don't appear to be able to do something until you have mastered the skill in private, and only then present it to the world. I all but skipped home.

Jessica told me about the other one years later.

At break time Lucy would walk around the playground wearing her anorak the wrong way round, with the hood down under her chin like a pouch, and her friends would put crisps and what have you in the hood for her to eat.

'Well, you never, ever give us money for crisps, Daddy, and people felt sorry for me.'

She might well have been appearing to tread water, but all the time she was deceiving us all. Even so, Michelle's image of my little Lucy wrapped around Elizabeth, just sitting and watching and thinking while classroom life went on still breaks my heart.

13

Now the girls were back at school, I began to ease myself back into work. After nearly two months away, it was a strange, unfamiliar world in which I felt I never really fitted, despite people's compassion towards me. For almost a year, I felt as if I were doing somebody else's job and hugely lacked motivation, which was unsettling because work is one of the things in life I do pretty well. But now I was leading two lives: Jeremy at home was very different from Jeremy at work.

Once of the first things I did once I was back at the BBC, I did as a favour for Lizzie. I had made a half-hearted promise to her that I would try to get her on *Woman's Hour* to talk about her book. I hate using contacts for personal favours, which is why I had been lukewarm about it, and I also thought that they probably wouldn't be all that interested in her book and, with her stammer, I feared that Lizzie would be a terrible interviewee. But I emailed Jenni Murray, the presenter of the programme, not really expecting a response. She promptly replied that it was already on the list of books the programme wanted to cover, but she hadn't associated it with Lizzie, or Lizzie to me, and that they would be very keen to have me on the programme. She asked me if I wanted to do the interview live or recorded. She would prefer to pre-record. Thank God. I was so nervous that if she had asked me, 'Jeremy Howe, what is your name?' I would have got the answer wrong. But, in the end, the piece went OK, and it made me feel good.

Work was only possible because we had a nanny. I had high expectations of Linda, but she never really lived up to them. She was good on paper, and not much use off it. She just wasn't the right choice. I think my expectations of a twenty-year-old having to deal with a family mired in grief were wholly unrealistic, but it was a struggle. It turned out there were so many days she couldn't do because of other commitments; she seemed to have no energy; she wore false fingernails (which impressed Jessica enormously); and sometimes she just didn't turn up, which meant Catherine and other friends had to fill the breach. Although she was very nice and very kind to the girls, they ran rings round her when she was there – but mostly she wasn't. At least that meant she was cheap – ish.

We had a sweet tin. So many people brought us sweets – they must have felt sorry for us – that I stored them in an old ice-cream tub, which Jessica and Lucy could open only on pain of death – or worse. One night I came home late feeling rather peckish and opened it – to find it empty. Next morning, over breakfast, I quizzed the girls.

'Oh yes. Last night Linda let us eat them all after supper,' said Jessica dutifully.

'Why?'

'Because Lucy was sad.'

'I started to feel sick, so I couldn't eat them all,' chimed in Lucy.

'So Linda and I finished them off between us.'

As I was now back at work almost full-time, there then began the painfully tricky juggling act all working mothers are familiar with. On the three days she looked after the girls, Linda would pick them up from school and they would either have friends round to play or take them to friends. She would bring them home and cook them supper (Jessica and Lucy liked her cooking), give them a bath, then get them ready for bed and read them a story. As Jessica and Lucy pretty well refused to have anyone but me read to them, this was somewhat unrewarding. I got the feeling they spent quite a lot of time parked in front of the television watching *The Jungle Book* for the thousandth time while she tidied up and sorted out her social life on our phone.

I would catch the 6.15 p.m. train from Paddington, which got me home just before 7.30. It really didn't matter if I was in the middle of a meeting – at twenty to six I would simply leave the office. I would walk down the corridor and, as I pressed the lift button, I would shed work and suddenly all the worries and anxieties about home would hit me.

I would get home, call out a hello and go straight upstairs. Lucy would be in the bottom bunk, Jessica, being the eldest, on top. I would kiss them and, while they hugged me to bits, would do a handover with Linda while they told me, in a torrent, all the day's news.

'Really . . . well done . . . full marks! . . . did she? . . . did he? . . . that was naughty of him . . . ugh, spinach.' And so on and so on.

Linda would call out from downstairs. 'Bye! See you tomorrow.'

'Bye, Linda!' we would chorus. And the front door would slam and they would wave her down the street from the bedroom window.

I would then settle the girls down and read them a bedtime story. I ransacked all Lizzie's children's books, stuff that no right-thinking man would read in a million years, frayed, broken-backed, much–read, jam-stained Puffins. Lizzie loved her books, and I loved reading them – *The Little House on the Prairie*, *The Railway Children*, *Ballet Shoes* and, of course, *Milly Molly Mandy*. Jessica drank them up. Lucy just gazed into space, tucked up under her duvet. What on earth was she thinking?

Then Jessica would say, 'Daddy, tell me a story about when you were a little boy.' And I would oblige.

There was the story about when we went to Swanage with my grandparents, when I was four, all dressed up smartly in my new school uniform, with my first ever pair of black lace-up shoes. We had arrived at the hotel, having travelled in a first-class carriage in a train hauled by a steam engine (Just how exciting was that? Just how old am I, for heaven's sake?), in time for a late lunch, where tomato soup was served as a starter. I had never had tomato soup before, and it was delicious (this was quite a miraculous discovery, as I disliked nearly all food apart from mashed-up banana and raspberry or blackcurrant jam – but NEVER strawberry – spread on sliced white bread), but my shoelace was undone and I asked my granddad to do it for me, because I hadn't yet learnt to tie my own. While I was distracted by him tying my laces extra tight, the waitress took away my half-finished bowl of soup. I was devastated. All week they served different soups – oxtail, vegetable, cream of chicken – all uniformly horrible. My mum told me not to worry, that we were bound to have tomato soup on the last day, the following Saturday. But we didn't. Thereafter, my mother bought every conceivable type of tomato soup on the market – but none was as delicious as that first ever tomato soup, not even Heinz. Not since that day have I ever had such a tasty bowl of soup – and they took it away from me.

'Tell us another one about when you were a little boy, Daddy. Please!'

'I don't know any more.'

'Daddy, tell us the one about you and the swing.'

'Ah yes. Me and the swing. Well, when I was a little boy we had a swing in the garden which Uncle Jonathan and I used to love playing on. Because he was bigger than me – he was nearly seven, so I was nearly four – he was always telling me to swing higher and higher, and even though I was a bit scared, I always did. One day he said wouldn't it be exciting to jump off the swing while it was really high. "But won't I get hurt?" "No, don't be silly. It'll be fun." Because he was my older brother and he was always right, I decided to try – and off I jumped and landed in a crumpled heap on the lawn. As I stood up – I was a bit groggy at this point – the swing came back and hit me bang on the head and I fell over again. I just lay there, and all I remember was Uncle Jonathan running indoors shouting, "Mummy! Mummy! I've killed Jeremy!"'

'Were you really dead, Daddy?'

'No, of course not, silly, otherwise I wouldn't be here, would I? But I had sort of knocked myself out, so Grandma ran out, dumped me in Auntie Philippa's push-chair – she was still a baby then – and rushed me round to the doctor's. I felt terrible – because only babies go around in pushchairs.'

'What about the time you went shopping for the duck. Go on, Daddy.'

'When I was ten and we were living without my father, your grandpa, and we were really hard up, as a special treat, Grandma decided we would have roast duck with orange sauce. We went into town – in the rain – to buy everything for lunch, and were waiting at the bus stop with all the bags of shopping. As the bus approached, my mother picked up one of the carrier bags, and because it was made out of paper – carrier bags were when I was a little boy – and the pavement had been wet, the bottom fell out and all the oranges and the duck fell out and bounced across the pavement into the road. The bus squashed the oranges flat. Luckily, Uncle Jonathan dashed into the gutter and scooped up the duck. But we didn't have money for more oranges, so we never had our duck à l'orange.'

I quickly ran out of new stories to tell. What I never quite sussed was that Jessica loved hearing the same ones over and over. Or ones about Mummy as a little girl – which were more difficult because, of course, I hadn't grown up with her.

After the stories, I would draw the skimpy curtains and put up an old blue sleeping bag, opened out, to black out the window (hmm . . . I wonder why we had never had the curtains lined?), and they would turn on their bedside lamps.

Then it was time for prayers. I can't remember where Jessica got the idea of prayers from, but it was certainly after Lizzie's death. I would stand beside her and she would kneel on her bunk, squeeze her eyes tight shut and put her hands together, with Banana Custard (the afore-mentioned gibbon) or Bobba (a teddy bear) clamped under her arm.

'Dear Lord, thank you for the nice day I have had today and thank you for looking after Lucy and me and Daddy and Maka and Deda and Grandma and Auntie Louise and Auntie Philippa and the cousins, and please look after them tomorrow and always. Can I speak to Mummy now? Hello Mummy, I had a nice day today, I hope you did too. Daddy got cross with Lucy at breakfast because she wouldn't eat her Cheerios. Catherine Unia took me and Lucy to school, and she got very cross with Joe because he found a squashed frog in the park and wanted to take it to show Mr Standish, but she wouldn't let him. We had a spelling test today and I got full marks. Only me and Charlotte got full marks. For lunch we had cottage pie and cabbage and I sat next to Becca, who made me cross because she was silly and wouldn't eat her cabbage. Linda picked us up from school and we went round to Suzy's, where we made animals from clay. Lucy made an elephant, but his trunk kept falling off. I made a bumble bee, but it wouldn't come out right, so I got cross. We had sausages for tea, I had three and Lucy only had one and then I spoke to Maka and then Lucy and me watched a bit of *Beauty and the Beast*. Tomorrow is Katie's little brother's birthday party. I am going to write my Christmas list soon. I want a Thumper Rabbit like Lucy's. Look after yourself and speak to you tomorrow. I love you lots, Mummy. Amen.'

It was an agonizing ritual we performed every night for years. And every night it wrung at my heart.

Lucy would never join in. Instead, she'd lie there and say something like, 'I don't need to speak to Mummy – she can see me through a window in heaven, so she knows what I have done today.'

Which is more than I knew, as she would never tell anyone. For example:

'Did you have a nice day at school today, darling?'

'Yes.'

'What did you do?'

'I can't remember.'

'Who did you sit next to in class?'

'Esther.'

'Is she your best friend?'

'Sometimes she is. Can I go and watch television now?' was a typical exchange with Lucy.

After the goodnight ritual, all I was fit for was a drink. But usually Lucy needed a wee and Jessica remembered she had not cleaned her teeth. One night, she proudly showed me her wobbly tooth.

'It'll soon be time for the tooth fairy.' She grinned at me and then looked worried. 'Daddy, I forgot to tell Mummy about my tooth. What shall I do?'

'Tell her tomorrow.'

'Oh. OK'

I would then put them down for the night. Jessica would only go to sleep if she knew I was downstairs, so the deal was that I would take Banana Custard downstairs with me and tuck it under her duvet next to her and Bobba once she was asleep. This was a high-risk strategy – it involved creeping upstairs every ten minutes to see if she was asleep, but, of course, if I disturbed her as I put the diminutive floppy gibbon next to her, her eyes would spring open and the whole process had to begin again (there are parallels here with defusing an unexploded bomb). Sometimes I would come up three or four times before she was settled. Or, even worse, I would FORGET and at about ten o'clock, a tearful Jessica would appear downstairs, weeping and accusing me of running away, etc., etc., and the whole palaver would begin again.

I would then close the bedroom door, leaving a crack of light from the hall, the size of the crack dictatorially determined by Jessica, who was afraid of the dark.

Sometime around eight-thirty, I would start cooking supper.

Sometime around eight thirty-five, I would sit down for supper (yes, my cooking was that good) with a glass of wine. I would always have the radio on. Radio 4 became my constant companion, my reliable friend. I have no idea what I was listening to; it just made the house less silent.

Eating a meal solo took about five minutes, with the *Guardian* as a readable table mat. My diet became a dull litany of the children's reheated leftovers, Sainsbury's microwaveable chicken pasta bake, a steak pie or pasta with pesto. Sometimes I would splash out and grill myself a pork chop. I existed on those incredibly expensive bags of pre-washed lettuce, because I couldn't be bothered with cooking vegetables. And a Müller Fruit Corner Black Cherry Yoghurt for pudding (for years they were three for the price of two). The taste of any of those things will instantly bring back the silence of the house in Oxford: lights burning everywhere to make the house feel less lonely (like Jessica, I too was afraid of the dark now, more afraid of it than the electricity bill even), the booming echo of our newly enlarged kitchen, the quietness of a family home emptied of family life, the creeping about so that I didn't disturb the girls whose lives I shared for an hour and a half every day. I camped in that house. I felt like an interloper. The only room that I liked was the girls' bedroom. It was the only room that felt like it was lived in. Our house was no longer our home. It had had the life sucked out of it. The only noise to be heard once the radio was silenced was a tap dripping – because I didn't know how to change the washer.

I would wash up after my supper and, at about nine o'clock, I would settle down to some work – invariably listening to a radio play that I had started listening to on the train home and had fallen asleep to. Or I would play chess against myself, or patience. And kill time.

One night the phone rang.

It was Maka. This was unusual. Unfailingly, she would phone the girls every evening after supper and want to hear about their day, and if I was at home I would talk to her, but if she phoned me, it was usually about what size clothes she should buy them, did I think they needed new shoes, when she should next come down to Oxford, etc., etc. She didn't really do small talk.

She immediately launched into some obscure stuff about inheritance and the children. I found I was struggling to understand. She wasn't being very clear, which was also unusual.

'I see . . . I see . . . ,' I said, but I am not sure that I did, and then she rang off.

I sat and pondered the import of what she'd said.

Shit.

I picked up the phone and dialled their number.
'Maka?'
'Yes?'
'I was just thinking about what you just said.'
'Yes.'
'Correct me if I am wrong, but what you have just tried to tell me is that you have written me out of your will.'
'Yes. That's right. Sorry if I wasn't very clear.'
'So – not that it is any business of mine – but not only have I just lost my wife, but you have taken away any financial safety net that being married to her gave me.'
'Yes. I suppose that is true. But our priority is to provide for the grandchildren.'
'Is that very fair on me? Is it that you don't trust me?'
Pause.
'That is what we have decided.'
'Why?'
'Well . . .'
'I feel hurt. Obviously it is your money and you need to do with it what you think fit, but let me just say how hurt I feel.'
'If that's the way you see it . . .'
'I do. I'm sorry, but there it is. I don't think there is anything more to be said, do you?'
'Um.'

'Goodnight, Maka.'

'Goodnight.'

Phone conversations don't come much more painful than that, to either party. I was upset. But who should I tell I was upset? The cat?

Naively, I had always seen myself as being as much their son as their son-in-law, simply an extension of their beloved daughter. Not only was this a body blow, but so too was the fact that another financial safety net had been swiped away from me at a point in my life when I needed all the security I could grab. Looked at rationally, it was a completely obvious thing for them to do – why on earth would they leave half of their estate to an outsider? – but we were not in a rational world. Nor did they really need to tell me. They could have written me out of their will and I need never have known. In telling me, they had undermined our relationship. Yes, it was the decent, honest thing to do – Maka was decent and honest to a fault – but it was insensitively handled. This may not seem like a big deal to you, but I felt not only as if a bond had been broken, but that bond had in fact been illusory. I had been deceiving myself that I was a son to them; now I knew that I was not. If only Maka had kept silent, I would have been none the wiser. Instead, by telling me, our relationship had been damaged irreparably.

All that said, Maka and Deda were still extremely generous: they paid for the girls' piano lessons, they bought them clothes. More significantly, they paid for the nanny, and Maka would come and stay to look after the children at the drop of a hat, no matter how painful living in her daughter's house without her daughter was to her. But nothing was the same as it had been before Lizzie died.

Lizzie and her mother had been very close. They'd speak nearly every day, and when the children were first born, she would come over and stay with us in Belfast for a week or two at a time. I liked her and we got on. She was fiercely intelligent, brisk to the point of rudeness and, like a lot of women of her generation – she was in her mid-sixties – had lived her life vicariously through her daughter's achievements, because she had never had the opportunities she had been able to give to her children.

She never recovered from her daughter's death – for nearly fifteen years, she got on with life just as before, largely uncomplaining, phoning the girls every day of their lives, doing *The Times* crossword and playing chess with herself. She read a crime novel a day, drank too much sherry, too much whisky, too much red wine and smoked too many fags. She was outwardly civil and content, but to me it seemed she was wearing a mask. After I gave her the appalling news about Lizzie, I only ever saw her really happy once. It was years later and she was lying on her deathbed after suffering a massive stroke. Her face was at rest, she looked contented. She had wanted to be with her beloved daughter since the day Lizzie died, and now she was about to join her.

It seems to me that, just as there are distinct phases of

grief, there are also three immutable, almost Newtonian laws of grief:

The First Law: I loved Lizzie with all my heart, but although it felt inconceivable at the time, there was always the possibility that I would find another partner. At the age of sixty-five, you cannot have another daughter. It is a loss you can never recover from.

The Second Law: people grow and change at different rates, mostly dependent on age. Lucy was four and Jessica six when their mother died. Six years later, when Jessica was twelve and Lucy was ten, both girls had lived half of their lives without her, and they were effectively different people. They had moved on simply by growing. Maka and Deda had lived less than a tenth of their lives in those six years and were still the same people they were when Lizzie died. They were mired in grief. They were in a terrible position, and although I could feel sorry for them, to be honest, I had too much to do in my own life to pay much attention.

And the Third Law: grief can pull people apart. All too often, you see families buckling under extreme grief. Show me a family who has suffered a public bereavement (the Lawrences, the Paynes, etc.) and five years on, the chances are that the mother and father have separated. In order to survive a tragedy, which is going to test you until you are at breaking point, you need very firm foundations.

Distressing telephone calls did not mark all my evenings. Mostly I would watch the *News at Ten* or *Newsnight* and go to bed at about eleven. I so couldn't sleep in our bedroom on my own that I had moved downstairs to the spare room, which was barely larger than a cupboard: there was only enough space for a small double bed and me. The walls were bare except for a print from Blake's illustrations of the Book of Job propped up against the wall (Job was a man with whom I empathized). It was my cell. Comfortless but for the bottle of whisky tucked under the bed beside a pile of unread books.

Another day over. Another day survived. Thank God. I too said my prayers – a grownup version of Jessica's, repeated like a protective mantra: 'Dear Lord, thank you for the day I have had today, thank you for looking after us, and please let tomorrow be another good day. Let Lizzie know that I love her and look after her. For Jesus Christ's sake, Amen.' I would list everybody who I wanted looking after as fast as possible and then slow down – and mouth the words – for the bit about Lizzie, just to feel her in my heart for as long as possible, like a burning sensation in my chest, a lump in my throat, a rush of blood to the head. It was all the emotion I allowed myself. It was so painful that I would try to get it over with as early before bed as possible – while cleaning my teeth, while going for a pee – rather than just before settling down to sleep. After what had happened to us I wasn't even sure I believed in God, but it was a kind of insurance policy. Then it would be a slug of whisky and lights out.

Damn! Banana Custard was still bloody well downstairs.

14

We struggled on and I managed to keep our heads above water. But it was tough going. We needed a miracle. To our relief, a miracle came, in the shape of Dr Forrest. She was some doctor, and meeting her was the third time the NHS had saved my bacon since Lizzie's death.

Good as her parting words when I had gone to see her about the children and the funeral, the head of child psychiatry in Norwich put us in touch with her opposite number in Oxford and towards the end of that weird school summer holiday, off we all three trooped to meet Dr Forrest.

She was the head of the Child Psychiatry Department at the Park Children's Hospital in Oxford. She was petite, smiling, with an intense, warm gaze, well-spoken, very smart (in all senses) and a few years older than me. In the movie, she will be played by Helen Mirren.

I don't know what she did for us, but the children loved visiting her and she always made me feel good about my role as a parent.

Which, of course, is what she did for us.

First thing every Friday morning for over a year, we

would park the car in the front of a large, rambling Victorian house turned into a hospital, go to the reception area in a boomy hall and be told to go upstairs and wait for Dr Forrest to collect us. We climbed the stairs, up and up, past classes of children – what were they in here for, what terrible fate had befallen them? I wondered – until we reached a gate at the top, in the attic space. We would sit on an NHS padded bench by the gate and wait; the ritual was to sit Jessica on one knee and Lucy on the other and play 'This is the way the lady rides, trot trot trot trot', joggling them gently up and down, getting more and more vigorous until: 'This is the way the kangaroo jumps, boing boing boing boing', which would all but throw them off my knees.

Then Dr Forrest would come and greet us, and we would troop into her large consulting room built into the eaves of the building. The girls would again sit on my lap, so I was almost hidden behind them, and Dr Forrest would ask them how they were.

'Fine, thank you, Dr Forrest,' they chorused.

'Well, actually, you haven't been sleeping too well, have you, Jessica?' I added.

'No. Lucy snores and keeps me awake.'

'I don't snore.'

'Well, she talks in her sleep.'

'I don't, Daddy, do I!?'

'No, darling, Jessica is talking rubbish.' And Jessica would giggle. She always has been the world's most pathetic fibber.

'I don't. Anyway, you snore, Daddy,' and then Dr Forrest would shift the squabble into why Jessica was having problems getting to sleep – because she was worried that I wasn't in the house, that I might disappear like Mummy did, and so on and so on. It was Dr Forrest who had come up with the nightly ritual with Banana Custard to put Jessica at ease about my being in the house; it was Dr Forrest with whom I discussed whether or not we needed to continue with her prayers.

'Now, girls, why don't you draw me a picture? You know where the crayons are.' They would scurry off and find pens and Dr Forrest would find important-looking documents, which they would draw all over the back of.

I had been worried that before Lizzie's death Jessica used to write stories and now she would not. The drawing was an attempt to get Jessica to start writing again. The only story she wrote for Dr Forrest was one called 'The Rainbow'. After three words – 'One day there . . .' – the story stopped. Instead, she now lay on the floor writing rows and rows of numbers. She didn't want to draw pictures anymore.

Lucy, on the other hand, drew all the time: Mummy standing on the grass in the sunshine with a big smile on her face. Next to her was what can only be described as a huge rabbit-like *Donnie Darko*-esque monster with arrows shooting out of it saying 'Lucy'; or a spindly Mummy picking flowers in a beautiful garden. She then changed the picture by placing Mummy in a massive, scribbled black frame that blotted out whole swathes of the garden, as if Mummy was in a Mark Rothko-like box.

I was disturbed by these.

'No, don't be, Mr Howe. Obviously the black box represents Lucy's Mummy's death – in your lovely picture, is the black because you are sad about your Mummy being dead, Lucy?'

An almost imperceptible nod from Lucy, who continued drawing for another few seconds, and then downed tools and came and snuggled onto my lap.

'But she has drawn Mummy in a lovely garden – aren't these flowers pretty, Lucy? Did your Mummy like picking flowers?'

Lucy nodded. Lizzie was a fervent picker of flowers.

'And are you sad that your Mummy is dead? Is that why you have drawn these big black lines around her?'

'Yes,' she said very quietly and gave me a cuddle.

'It is the saddest thing in the world, isn't it, Lucy? Everybody is very sad that your Mummy is dead.'

'At Mummy's funeral EVERYBODY was crying,' chimed in Jessica while she scribbled away on the floor at her number grid.

'Well, everybody was so sad to see your Mummy dead. She was a very special and lovely Mummy. You are right to feel sad, Lucy.' Pause. 'Do you want to play with the Playmobil, Lucy? Why don't you get it out for you and Jessica.'

And Lucy slipped off my knee and, with Jessica's help,

got out the biggest, most wonderful Playmobil set ever, with schools and farms and families with children and firemen, astronauts, Playmobil politicians and Playmobil terrorists . . . well, you name it, Dr Forrest's Playmobil had it. If you are not a Playmobil aficionado, you will have no idea what I am talking about, but my two loved the bendy plastic figures with big heads who slotted neatly into furniture and stuff. Dr Forrest had the Playmobil set to end all Playmobil sets, and she knew it, and would play it as her trump card. Lucy was instantly happy as she and Jessica clucked and cooed and scrabbled over setting up a Playmobil hospital with doctors and nurses and an operating table – it probably had Playmobil spare organs – while Dr Forrest and I continued discussing the pictures and the openness of the girls to discussing their emotions with me.

'A lot of children who come to see me just cannot bear to draw a picture of their dead parent. All they can do is scribble. That Lucy is drawing pictures of her mother in such a lovely space is an incredibly good sign. Her memories are good ones and she can express them freely. Honestly, Mr Howe, that is such a good thing.'

Too quickly – for both the girls and for me – our precious hour would be up. The girls would pack up the Playmobil and the pens, Dr Forrest would ask if she could keep the pictures and we would arrange another session. I remember once, when I was feeling particularly hopeless about my parenting skills, as we left the room, she just whispered to me, 'Mr Howe, you are doing just brilliantly.' No one has ever given me greater praise. Just seven words – but seven words that utterly transformed how I felt about myself as a parent.

'In child psychiatry, we always say that the first four years of good parenting are worth money in the bank and, Mr Howe, your two girls have gold in their bank.'

For that, I loved Lizzie more than ever. I think it is the valediction she would have prized above everything else: that as a mother she had put gold in her children's bank.

Session over, we would race downstairs to the hospital lobby, where on either side of the busy corridor stood two of the largest, handsomest rocking horses ever made. They were the quintessence of rocking horse, the platonic model for all rocking horses. Jessica would clamber up onto hers (on the left) and I would lift little Lucy onto the one on the right and they would gallop away on them for ten minutes, riding all the cares of the world away. 'Time' – being ever the enemy in life – 'to get to school, girls.'

'Just one more minute, Daddy, please.'

'One minute, and no more,' as I got out my car keys threateningly, and they would gallop away over the last furlong of their imaginary race course and then I would drive them to school, take them late into class and then go to work myself, very, very late.

On one occasion I wanted Jessica to see Dr Forrest by herself – she had such anxieties about being apart from me and I felt that with me in the room she would never talk to

Dr Forrest. Dr Forrest probed and probed, ever so gently and sweetly.

'You know what, Jessica? I don't think you want to see me on your own. But maybe the next time you come, how about if your Daddy was to sit outside while you and I have a little chat together?'

Jessica clearly thought this was a pants idea, but she was so in thrall to Dr Forrest that she grudgingly agreed to her suggestion.

Next Friday, we took Lucy to school and then Jessica and I drove up to the hospital. It felt a bit strange. While we waited for Dr Forrest, she sat silently on my lap, as if clamped to me. She didn't want to play 'This is the Way the Lady Rides'. When Dr Forrest welcomed us, Jessica held my hand as tightly as she possibly could and all but dragged me into the consulting room. It was obvious to both Dr Forrest and me that she was not going to be parted from me, so the deal was that she would sit on my lap and I would remain silent while she and Dr Forrest chatted.

When I say chatted, I mean Jessica remained silent while Dr Forrest and I talked. Apart from the occasional mumbled grunt, Jessica didn't really join in, despite Dr Forrest's best endeavours. As this agonizing session drew to a close:

'Do you know what I think, Jessica?'

Pause. Jessica looked at her anxiously with big eyes and mouthed a silent 'No.'

'I think your coming to see me works best when you

and Lucy and Daddy are here all together. So next time you visit, why don't all three of you come?'

Game, set and match to Jessica Howe. She chatted to me all the way to school.

15

'I think you are underskilled in the washing, ironing and cooking departments,' was what the next miracle who came into my life – one Dr John Hall – told me on our first meeting. I needed counselling, not just for my family, but for myself. Collectively, our heads were above water, but I was not coping. Admitting this was a big deal, a bit like saying that I was an addict. My GP, who was very sympathetic, suggested I try a bereavement counsellor at Cruse. 'I can tell one thing, Mr Howe,' the counsellor said, after I had blubbed through my one and only session there, 'that you are sad. Very sad.'

'I did wonder if they might find you a bit of a challenge,' said my GP. 'Ask Dr Forrest if there is anyone that she knows. I will happily refer you.'

I asked her. She was hesitant. 'I will give it some thought.' As this particular session had been before term time started, I had taken the children shopping for shoes before returning home. I could do shoes, I could do underwear, but I didn't have the confidence to do clothes. In fact, I never really bought them any clothes, except for at Gap sales (i.e. nothing very girly!) – they were dressed in hand-me-downs from friends or in presents from Maka. My sister Philippa, who was staying with us, told me I had just missed a call from a John Hall, who had said that he might be able to help me.

'I told him you didn't just need any old help, that awful things had happened to you. I asked him if he had any experience in counselling people in your situation.'

'And?'

'He said he had. He told me he was the head of the Clinical Psychology Department at the Warneford Hospital.'

'Blimey. I'd better phone him then.'

At our first meeting he kind of auditioned me, said I shouldn't think of him as a crutch, and for half an hour seemed pretty reluctant to commit to seeing me even to the end of the appointed session. But finally he agreed to see me on a regular basis. I felt pleased with myself that I was clinically mad enough to have passed my interview.

'I think I can be of some help,' he told me before going on to give me his low opinion of my domestic skills. I had visions of him teaching me how to iron shirt collars, but in fact he was fabulously helpful.

Whenever I think of John, I think of Margaret Thatcher's quiet nemesis, Geoffrey Howe – grey, slightly portly, very measured and calm. The big difference was that John's initial toughness masked real compassion and gentleness. I don't think you could accuse Sir Geoff of being either compassionate or gentle.

John told me that I had lost my map, that his job was to help me re-find my bearings and the path that I had mislaid. His judgement had a clarity about it that was both helpful and comforting: he was dead right – I lived day by day, and could no longer plan for, or even conceive of, a future. Six months after I began seeing him, I woke up one morning and realized how much I was looking forward to Easter – nearly three weeks away – because Lucy's godfather Eoin was taking us all to Spain. It was an amazing breakthrough, because before that all I had been able to do was plan the children's childcare for a week. John was gradually guiding me towards seeing that there was a future.

When I first saw him, I was sleeping badly. He sat and thought for a few moments. 'How old is your duvet?'

'I dunno. Lizzie and I must have bought it when we moved into a flat with a double bed. About ten years old, I guess.'

'I think on Saturday you should go to Debenhams and buy a new one, a thicker one.'

'Why?'

'Two bodies sleeping together create a lot more heat than one. Now you are sleeping alone, you need a decent duvet.'

Ever the rebel, I, of course, bought it from M&S, but he was right. I started to sleep through the night because I was warm.

He suggested that I bought the smaller bed.

I told him about how badly I thought I had been treated

by the police, how I felt that the Open University had been neglectful and careless of my feelings and how damaged I felt by this.

'These are sins of omission, they are people not meeting the standard of behaviour you are entitled to, but in comparison with the sin of commission – the murder of Lizzie – Jeremy, they are inconsequential. Treat them as such. Get over them, push them to one side.'

Or, to put it another way: get a grip, man, and save your anger for the person who most deserves it, the man who murdered Lizzie.

He was right. It calmed me down.

It was he who – by deduction – told me why Robin Pask had killed Lizzie: he was a schizophrenic for whom there was no cure.

He advised me to stop thinking about the family that Pask had left behind – 'You have only so much compassion. Focus your real compassion on those who need you, not those you can do nothing about.'

I told him that my grief felt like an infinite black hole which was swallowing up my whole life. 'The hole may be huge or it may be small,' he told me, 'but let's define it, work out how big it is for you. Then you may wish to look into the hole or you may want to put a fence around it and ignore it.' He was right – if you try to get the measure of something, it becomes much easier to deal with. He taught me how to cope.

'I sense that you fear going back to York,' he told me.

'I'm never going there again if I can help it.'

'You have to put returning to York on your agenda. It doesn't matter if it is next week, next year or next century, one day you need to go back to York on your own volition. Right now I don't think you can, but one day, for business or some such, you might be called on to go. Don't let that ambush you. And besides, this year it's York you can't visit, next year Yorkshire, then the north of England, until eventually you will become trapped in your house.'

He developed strategies with me so that I could handle birthdays, Christmas, the impending trial, the anniversary of Lizzie's death, Valentine's Day, Mother's Day and all the other death traps that the calendar presents to the bereaved. He eased me back into the real world and helped rub out the chalk circle that was isolating me.

Initially we met two, sometimes even three, times a week and then, like a heroin addict in rehab, I was eased off our meetings. After two years, it was time to part.

'Jeremy, what you have been through is acute posttraumatic stress.'

I felt a bit cheated. Why hadn't he told me this when we first met? It all seemed so obvious, so easy to define. As I was wading through grief, unable to work out why I was feeling so inadequate, so directionless, telling me this might have helped me find my compass. But I realized that when we started our sessions, even if John had told me, I was so far from the mountaintop that any information that he might have given me on how to get there would not have helped. I couldn't – then – understand what I was going through, let alone see the road ahead. It is a commonplace that time is a healer, which is very true, I think – time certainly helped to heal me, but with a lot of assistance from men of medicine.

16

This is the story of a typical weekend with the Howes.

It was November 1992. A Saturday.

I woke up. As it was a lie-in day, I was up and washed and dressed and fearfully crotchety by about a quarter to eight.

I started off trying to be nice to the children: I brought them juice, I asked them how they'd slept, what they'd dreamt about (Lucy: 'Nothing. I was asleep'), even suggested what they should wear. But by about a quarter to eight I was nagging them to get up, get dressed and get ready, because—

<u>Saturday is the day we go to Sainsbury's.</u>

And if we didn't get there by nine o'clock it would be full of people, and much as I dislike supermarkets, I am phobic about supermarkets with people in them.

Jessica was quite amenable; Lucy was just grumpy and uncooperative. God knows why because they would get to choose a cake each. And if they were really good, I would let them push the trolley (even though I have to admit to quite liking pushing it myself).

The supermarket was empty.

I didn't have a list. That would be too anally retentive. I am a man. When I arrived I felt quite upbeat, but by the time I'd got through the forbidding barrier of fruit and veg at the entrance, I had lost the will to live and, sensing this, the children scurried off to choose a breakfast cereal.

Every week Lucy tried to inveigle me into buying Coco Pops. Every week, unless it was one of their birthdays, I got them Weetabix, because I naively thought that it didn't have any added sugar. Lucy hated Weetabix. We had more rows about Weetabix than about anything else.

'So what do you want?'

'Coco Pops.'

'But you can't have Coco Pops. What do you want if you can't have Coco Pops?'

Pause.

'Coco Pops.'

'Lucy, why don't you choose Cheerios. Because Daddy won't let you have Coco Pops.'

'But I like Coco Pops.'

'But you do like Cheerios, Lucy,' mediated Jessica.

I went off to hunt for tea bags (decaff) and let them fight it out.

I returned to find Coco Pops in the trolley and the girls hopping about on either foot, hoping I wouldn't notice.

'But you can't have Coco Pops, Lucy,' as I put them back on the shelf.

'But I like Coco Pops.'

After another hour or so of wrangling, Jessica talked

Lucy into choosing Rice Krispies. I mean, they are the same as Coco Pops – well, nearly. It's just they are not covered in chocolate. 'They are just as nice. Really.' And I chucked in a box of Rice Krispies, thus deferring the row until Monday morning.

By then I was exhausted, pushing a trolley full of inedible garbage that no one liked, except for two gingerbread men, which we always got and which always took about fifteen minutes to choose.

'No, that one please, not that one,' said Lucy, who I was holding up to the glass counter.

'This one?' asked the man serving us.

'No, er . . .'

'This one?'

'No, that one. That one there.' She pointed rather vaguely and desperately.

'I think she means this one, with red, yellow and blue Smarties for buttons, not the one with the three orange ones.' Whoever heard of a child wanting matching colours when they could have lots of different ones? Clearly the man behind the counter had never met a child. Pah.

'Thank you, Daddy.' And she held my hand tightly and flushed pink. The way to a child's heart is through coloured Smarties.

After about a hundred years lost in the aisles and reefs of the supermarket, we reached the checkout. The thought of having to unpack all this stuff onto the checkout belt, only to re-pack it into the trolley, only to load it into the car, where everything would fall out of the bags, only to unload it and then unpack it at home was dispiriting, especially as I could now see what I had bought and what I had forgotten. I ran off to get instant coffee (decaff), leaving Jessica and Lucy at the checkout, obviously not having taken heed of the lurking child abductors of Ian McEwan's *The Child in Time* (I just didn't have the time to take heed).

I had become a useless shopper. Which I didn't understand, because I used to do the Saturday shop when Lizzie was alive. I actually used to quite enjoy it – it was quality time with the children, albeit in Sainsbury's. Now I seemed to spend huge amounts of money on food that no one liked. After several years of listless consumption, one of our nannies made me compile a shopping list on my computer. It took all the fun out of shopping , but it did mean we actually got what we needed.

Having achieved all of the above, I flopped down at home with a cup of coffee (decaff) and a sticky Belgian bun. It was not yet ten o'clock, and I had the whole day ahead of me, but I was knackered. I wished it was bedtime already. Why?

Because I had my regular Saturday migraine coming on. Before Lizzie died, I didn't know what migraines were. Now, without fail, every Saturday, I would get a pain like someone was screwing a vice onto my temples. My brain would slow down so that I slurred my speech and I would feel tired, irritated and nauseous, with a heightened sense of smell (Mrs Singh was preparing curry ten doors away –

I could smell it from our kitchen with my migraine on) and a suicidal craving to eat chocolate. My body was willing me to lie down.

I felt so guilty – I should have been playing with the girls and instead I was phoning Julia across the road to see if she could look after them while I went to bed. No answer. I tried Suzy. No answer. Christiana; no answer. Catherine was at work.

The doorbell rang.

It was Julia. Thank God. She was on her way back from the shops and wondered if the girls would like to come over to do some cooking. Maybe I would like to pop round for some lunch later, say in a couple of hours. Jessica and Lucy thought this was a brilliant idea, so I walked over with them, idly chatted with Julia on her doorstep, rushed back home, took half a sleeping tablet, set the alarm for a couple of hours later and tried to sleep off my headache.

My alarm went off. Sluggishly, the pain in my head having receded, I got up. I attempted to tidy up some of our domestic chaos, then wandered over to Julia's, where family life was in full swing and Jessica and Lucy were baking, as at home there as they were in our house. Jessica was busy bossing Harry and Edie around and Lucy came and snuggled on my lap to draw a picture while Julia cooked lunch and her husband Ollie pottered around in a DIY kind of way.

'What have you drawn, darling?'

'A picture.'

'That's really nice. What is it?' A huge head filled the paper. It had tiny features and a large, smiling mouth.

'It's a picture of you.'

'Oh, that's nice, darling. Why have I got such a big head and two tiny bodies?'

'Because you are my Mummydaddy,' and she laughed and turned pink.

I've still got that drawing. In fact, it was almost what gave me the idea for this book. Lucy had summed up my challenge as a parent and my qualities as one succinctly and brilliantly. I wasn't Mummy (how could I be?) and I wasn't just Daddy anymore. I was, simultaneously, Mummydaddy.

We lunched as a family, then the girls went off to play with Harry and Edie while Julia, Ollie and I chatted over coffee. I was always clock-watching. I always felt like an imposition, never wanting to outstay my welcome, but always keen to stay, not to kill time, but to feel a part of a normal family life. I found a lot of surrogate families that year, they were a lifeline. They helped me feel like part of the human race. And, boy, did I learn the meaning of 'singing for your supper' – I would try never to bore my hosts, would tell funny stories, do the washing up, make coffee, entertain them as best I could and never unburden on them my multiple woes. I so hope that all those generous people didn't feel I leeched off them.

After being fed, watered and generally looked after, we'd go home and the children would settle down for a good long play.

'We're going upstairs to play the Anna game, Daddy.' Or 'Do we have to go out? We are in the middle of the Anna game.' Or 'Don't disturb us, Daddy, we are just coming to the best bit of the Anna game.'

The origins of the Anna game are lost in the mists of time. It appeared to have no start, no middle and no end, and I have no idea who Anna is or was, but it absorbed the children. My anthropological observations revealed that it could only really be enacted in their bedroom, behind closed doors, that it was a make-believe game, and that it chiefly consisted of getting a lot of props together and playing out any one of about a million scenarios (for example, after returning home from a holiday abroad, it would chiefly consist of the girls playing at air hostesses; when a friend of ours took them to the ballet, the Anna game became a dance class, etc.). Dressing up in their mother's clothes – which were still hanging in the wardrobe opposite their room – was mandatory. Whenever I eavesdropped, I mostly heard Jessica ordering her sister about – 'Now, Lucy, you've got to do it like this . . .'

If I ventured into their room they would stop and Jessica would say, with a big grin on her face, 'We're busy with the Anna game, Daddy. We can't be disturbed because we are busy stamping library books. Unless you would like to borrow some?'

'That's a good idea. I need some new books to read.'

Then I would discover that the rules for borrowing books were so stringent and complicated that Lucy would have to choose them for me and Jessica, as the bossy librarian, would have to tell me off.

They would break off midway, come down for juice and a biscuit and talk excitedly about how they were now busy putting on a play in the Anna game and it was *The Sleeping Beauty* and they were just having a rest, but when it was ready would I like to see the dance bit?

After a couple of hours of this, they would come down and watch the video of *The Little Mermaid*, exhausted, while I made an attempt at cooking supper, usually involving a grill or the microwave and me getting very ratty as nothing ever seemed to cook at the same speed, and always served up with raw sliced red pepper and carrots. 'Beans or frozen peas?' I would yell out. 'Do we have to?' came the inevitable response. I was eventually rescued from cooking hell by my sister giving me Delia Smith, so that I could spend an entire afternoon failing to make a tasty spaghetti bolognaise or pork stew, but at least with Delia I kind of knew what I was supposed to be doing. There must be one or two other dishes I learnt to cook apart from spaghetti bolognaise, but I am blowed if I can remember what.

I'd wash up, they'd put away, and then we would settle down for a game – Frustration or Sorry or Uno.

Bath, bed, story, prayers, all done to a rigorous timetable – supper at six, game at six-thirty, bath at seven (it was a weekend so they could stay up, mmm, at least fifteen minutes later than usual), lights out at a quarter to eight. An unwavering timetable – a structure and a timetable somehow kept me going, kept me sane, as if I were running some endless race against a clock – and then the rest of the evening was mine, in which to feel like a spare part. Without the girls or my work, I just did not exist.

Sunday was completely different. Everything was closed – or at least things opened late and closed early – so there was less opportunity for trips out to shops or a cafe to distract us. Sunday is a family day, and we weren't really a family, more a husk of one. Families spend Sundays together, so there were rarely any casual drop-ins by friends or neighbours to while away our time, and I felt uneasy about just dropping in on them. I was on my own, unless I'd had the wit to organize something (unlikely) or some kind-hearted person had invited us somewhere (quite likely).

Sundays could be the best of days (if we had an outing) or the worst (if we didn't), and I became acutely aware of what, as a family, we had lost. I'm certain that one of the reasons any of us get married or find a partner is to make Sundays less of a hill to climb.

But Sundays were also a lie-in day. So, at about half past seven, Jessica would pad into my bedroom and ask if she and Lucy could watch children's television. I would get them juice and peanut butter (wholefood organic, of course, in deference to their mother) on cracker bread, settle them down in front of the telly and go back to bed to snooze for half an hour or so. The days of the long Sunday lie-in had disappeared with the advent of babies, and even today – twenty-five years after Jessica's birth – I find it almost physically and morally impossible to sleep much beyond eight.

To give the morning focus, I invented a big new ritual. We'd get up, have breakfast and then go to the Didcot Wave. And get there before it was full of people. You may have noticed that I have a fear of crowds.

As a child, I remember being taken swimming to Woolwich Baths most Sunday mornings, and although I found the swimming bit hard work, I loved the journey to and from the pool because we were driven by a friend and, as at that time we didn't have a car, this was a big treat. On the way home we would usually drive the back way across the Abbey Wood marshes, which until ten years before had been firing ranges and ammunition dumps for the Woolwich Arsenal, and it was an eerie and fascinating wasteland (it is Thamesmead now; not much change then), particularly for a boy from the boring suburbs. Sometimes, if we were lucky, we would be stopped by a train trundling past on the level crossing, the kind of thing that made a seven-year-old boy's day. And an even bigger treat was that after swimming, hair wet, wrapped up warmly against the cold, we would troop into a sweet shop by Abbey Wood station and my mother (never my father – he didn't come; in fact, I often wonder if my mother was having an affair with the guy who took us swimming) allowed us to choose a sixpence worth of sweets each, which for some unfathomable reason were called fairy sweets. Heaven indeed!

I tell you all this because I kind of replicated those

swimming expeditions for us three. Compared with Oxford, Didcot is the arse end of the world, a kind of frontier town built around a railway junction and a power station; the Dodge City of Oxon, our version of Abbey Wood. The whole swimming experience seemed to be one of coldness and chlorine, just like my childhood.

The first time we went to the baths a problem presented itself – where should we get changed? Family rooms hadn't yet been invented. I started off by taking them to the men's changing rooms, but somehow the girls getting undressed in front of loads of strangers with big, fat, hairy bellies and dangling cocks didn't feel right, so once Lucy could dress herself, the girls would troop off to the ladies' changing rooms and I would go to the men's. I could see that it made them feel terribly grown up, whereas I just felt wretched and lonely. I desperately wanted to follow them. I was still so unsure of their safety (why? Just how many child abductions take place in ladies' changing rooms in municipal baths per year in the UK? Mind you, how many women are stabbed to death on British university campuses in broad daylight?). It was like leaving them to go into a forbidding and forbidden city. And it felt all wrong. I'd get changed in about thirty seconds, even though I dawdled, whereas it seemed to take Jessica (chatting, as ever) and Lucy (slowcoach) about thirty minutes before they would appear by the poolside and scamper up to me, Lucy replete with armbands; Jessica, a proud swimmer (with a badge sewn onto her costume by Maka), without.

I would try to smile and be nice, but inside I was a bundle of irritation, anxiety and boredom – and then, of course, we had to go swimming.

To say that Mr Howe swims like a fish is a bit wide of the mark – I got my twenty yards certificate at school aged ten, and that was that. I have the natural buoyancy of concrete, and although I find swimming in the sea irresistible for up to five minutes (as long as it's shallow and warm), water is not my natural habitat. The good thing about going to the baths with a non-swimmer (i.e. Lucy) is that you have to stay in the shallow end. I do like my feet to be able to touch the bottom. We would play tag and have races (I am a fast swimmer over short distances – say six or seven feet) and mess about and wait for the wave machine, which was fun, and then I would start to get a bit cold and a bit grumpy and be angling to go, to tick the next thing off on my imaginary list of things to do to fill Sunday, and the girls would be angling to stay, and eventually I would win, and we would part at the communal footbath. I would dawdle again, and get showered and changed in about thirty seconds, feeling even more like a spare part as I watched fathers and sons get changed. The girls would take for ever, again (Jessica busy talking, Lucy a slow-coach), and after several epochs of hanging about in the dullest place ever conceived (the entrance lobby), my two would appear, brushing their long, wet hair, chattering away like teenagers, not a care in the world.

Into the car, wet towels in the boot, and then we would

stop for Sunday Sweets – something that would never have happened under the former regime, as their mum was an E-number/sugar fascist. Daringly, I now allowed the girls a bar of chocolate each. Please note the subtle name change from the fairy sweets of my childhood. I would stop the car, tell them I would be just a moment, lock them in, dash into the shop, always keeping them in my eyeline, buy the *Sunday Times*, a bar of chocolate for me (adult size) and one each for them (child size) and dash back. Amazingly, they were still safe, and probably hadn't even noticed that I was gone. I just didn't have the patience to spend half an hour unbuckling them from their seats, shepherding them into the shop and then leisurely reading the news, sport and arts sections of all the Sundays while they agonized over how to spend their fifteen pee, so I did it for them. For four years I did everything on the run.

The first time I did it, I felt dreadfully guilty about buying them sweets at all. And the look on their faces when I handed the booty over was one of astonishment.

'Jessica, Lucy – look what I have got you.' Through the car window, I waved two micro-sized chocolate Animal Bars, Lucy's with an elephant (her favourite animal) on the wrapper, Jessica's with a giraffe (they don't do bees – she loved bees, possibly because they were the only animal she could draw).

'Are they for us?'

'Yes. A treat.'

'Really?'

'Yes. Really.'

'Thank you, Daddy! Thank you!'

They clutched them as if they were gold ingots.

'Eat them now if you want,' I said, as I bit off a chunk of Mars Bar (I was allowed to eat sweets without permission from anyone, they weren't – isn't that the best thing about being grown up?).

'What, now? Oooh, THANK YOU, Daddy!' And gingerly they unwrapped their treasure, not quite believing what had just happened.

I have no idea how children can make such a small bar of chocolate last for so long, or how Lucy could get so much of it smeared round her mouth. I soon began to realize why mothers have so many paper hankies stashed up their sleeves, why they have handbags – mostly filled with wet wipes and Calpol and sticking plasters and safety pins. If you were to go through the pockets of my old jackets, you would be guaranteed to find them stuffed with screwed up paper hankies, sticky plastic medicine spoons and broken hair clips.

After the sweet shop, we'd head home down the dual carriageway at breakneck speed, as if I were in a race, a race against time. I set targets for everything – unrealistic ones, of course – back by ten-thirty, when we didn't leave the baths until twenty past ten, that kind of thing. Although I was driving, it was as if I were driven.

Sweets, drive, home – if possible in time to listen to the second half of *The Archers*, not because I was an addict, but because, as managing editor, it was my job – flop with the papers while the children played.

And then, almost inevitably, I'd remember an errand we needed to do. This particular weekend it was a birthday present for Jessica's friend Charlotte. Should we rush up to town now or wait until after lunch when it would be crowded?

'Jessica, Lucy, shall we go into town to get Charlotte's birthday present?'

'We're busy, Daddy,' came the cry. I capitulated and continued reading the papers.

We had an early lunch – peanut butter, crackerbread, carrot sticks and some salami and yoghurts – and then I drove up to town. We could have walked, but I hadn't got an hour to spend dawdling. We had one hour's parking in which to buy Charlotte a present – we headed straight for the Early Learning Centre, chose a drawing kit and were out in about seven minutes. Then we went to the card shop (which took two minutes) and then the Nosebag cafe, where I had a coffee and the girls had juice and we shared a Bakewell tart.

We were chatting away about how much Mummy liked to come up to town, come here and pretend to read a book and just people-watch, when an elderly Indian man leant over towards us and said to the girls, 'I remember your mother. She used to come and sit here and read on a Sunday afternoon. She was a lovely lady.'

We talked to him, and it really was Lizzie he was

talking about. Here was a random stranger who had a link to our past, a man who knew about us. It was a magical ten minutes. Lizzie was suddenly real and, as he spoke, the girls' eyes got bigger and bigger.

Our parking was about to run out, so we said our farewells and left. As they clambered down the cafe stairs, the girls were full of him: 'Daddy! Daddy! He knew Mummy! Was Mummy famous, Daddy?'

'No, my sweets, she was just Mummy.'

Mummy never wanted to be famous.

'But people know all about our Mummy! She wasn't just an ordinary Mummy, was she, Daddy?'

'No, my sweetie pets, she wasn't.'

'She was a special Mummy!'

'I know. Aren't you lucky to have had a Mummy like that?'

As we walked back to the car – or rushed because of the parking meter – Lucy suddenly exclaimed, 'Look! There's Mummy!'

I stopped, stunned. It was as if I had been hit by something. 'Where, darling?!' I searched the street. For a moment I believed Lucy.

Once Harry from across the road had found twenty pee in a gutter. Ever since, Lucy's eyes had been trained at her feet, looking for treasure – and now she had found some, of a kind. Lying in the gutter was a copy of Friday's *Oxford Mail* and there, on the front page, was a photograph of Lizzie side by side with an out-of-focus one of her killer being led into court in a bright-orange prison jumpsuit.

His trial date in the spring – nine months after Lizzie's death – had been announced the day before.

That image summed it all up – Lizzie lying discarded in the gutter, half fêted, half forgotten, her destiny yoked to an anonymous, blurred stranger whom I never wanted to have anything to do with. Since she'd died, I had desperately tried to separate Lizzie and her life from the manner of her death. It was a superhuman task, and here they were, randomly paired in a gutter, Lizzie and her murderer. It felt horribly public and horribly careless.

Years later, I searched the cuttings archive high and low for that edition of the paper, but could never find it. I sometimes wonder if we had all imagined it.

In the end, the waves on the beach will wash away everything.

'So Mummy *is* famous, Daddy!'

I was giddy with emotion.

'Not really, darling. Not really.' I had a lump in my throat and I could barely talk. Jessica squeezed my hand as we walked on in silence, but Lucy was skipping because she had found her Mummy, who was famous.

And then, just like all our Sundays, we went home, took a walk in the park, with the girls on their bicycles, a play on the swings and maybe a chat with a mum on a similar errand, followed by a futile attempt to do something about the morass of weeds that we called the back garden.

And then a supper of chicken drumsticks and baked potatoes in their jackets and bed – for them.

The bit of the weekend I looked forward to the most was nine o'clock on a Sunday evening, with the children tucked up and fast asleep and me spark out on the sofa. I would then hear feet padding up the path and a knock at the door and a voice calling, 'It's only me.' It was Catherine Unia, our child minder. On Sunday evenings I would pay her wages and we would spend an hour or so reviewing the week just gone and previewing the week ahead.

When we had moved to Oxford, Jessica and Lucy had been the first two children Catherine took on as a child minder and she had continued to look after them since, filling the very necessary gaps left by my not being able to afford – or find – Mary Poppins. I'd drop the girls off at her house after breakfast and either she or Linda would pick them up after school. She was always there as our backstop. She was a godsend, not a word I use carelessly. Oh, and did I mention that she was a qualified doctor, who had taken a break from doctoring to bring up her family of six children, one of whom was adopted, and that on Saturdays she ran a family-planning clinic? She was married to Pram, whose family had come to the UK from India via Kenya. They had met when he was a bus conductor in Cambridge and she a newly quali-fied doctor in Birmingham. He was now a senior manager in the Overseas Department of Oxfam, and thus spent nearly half the year in places like Afghanistan. Their eldest daughter Hannah was sitting her GCSEs, their youngest was a baby. Her son Joe was in Jessica's class at school. He was a cheeky monkey, but there was nothing about Joe not to like.

The Unias were an extraordinary family. Each one of them, in their way, held out a lifeline for us. But chief amongst them was Catherine. She was a year or two older than me, tall, floor-length, billowy, earth-mother skirts, long hair that hid her smiley eyes. She rarely made eye contact and was actually quite shy despite her extrovert manner. She was fabulously judgemental, gossipy, fiercely principled and fundamentally atheist. Yet she is the closest I have come to meeting a saint.

The story of the adoption says everything you need to know about the Unias. Catherine was about four months pregnant with child number three (soon to be known as Emily), a white woman living in India, where Oxfam had sent Pram. He came home and said, 'The nuns have asked me if we can find a home for a baby girl.' They could, and Martha joined the family.

Catherine sat down on the sofa in our sitting room, calendar in hand.

'Would you like a glass of wine?' I asked, as I went to the kitchen to get the money I owed her from last week's child-care and my calendar, on which was writ our weekly destiny.

'I'd rather have a beer,' she called out, and we settled down, drinks in hand, to organize my life for the next seven days.

'Well, how has it been this week?'

'I got through it.'

'I thought the girls had a good week. Jessica is really getting on with Katie.'

'Just because she can boss her around! But why does Jessica have to be so clingy every morning and Lucy so grumpy?'

Weekday mornings were not our best time. An average breakfast chez Howe would go like this:

I'd get the girls up; Jessica would be bouncy, Lucy grumpy. They'd choose their clothes, while I bathed, shaved and dressed, and then we all went down for breakfast: cereal, toast and juice. Jessica would munch her way through her Weetabix (see Sainsbury's, above) talking nineteen to the dozen about nothing very much in particular, probably about Katie, 'who is my best friend and I hate her' or Becca, 'who is just a pain'. Lucy sat stirring her Rice Krispies (see above also) idly with a spoon, daydreaming.

'Lucy, eat up, sweetie, we have to go to Catherine's in a minute.'

'I don't like Rice Krispies.'

'But you chose them, darling.'

'But I don't like Rice Krispies.'

'Lucy, you had better eat them up or Daddy will get cross with you,' her sister chipped in unhelpfully.

'But I don't like them.'

'Eat five more big spoonfuls and then we'll call it quits. OK, sweetie?'

'But I'm not hungry.'

I was busy cutting up an apple into slices for Jessica. 'Would you like some of Jessica's apple?'

'I don't like apples,' she whined. Jessica chomped on her apple slices ostentatiously.

'But, Lucy, you like apples really.'

'No, I don't,' and she plonked her spoon down defiantly.

I picked up Lucy's spoon and filled it to the brim with Rice Krispies. 'Come on, Lucy. Five big mouthfuls. I won't let you leave here without eating some breakfast.' Breakfast was the holy of holies for me. After all, you can't go to work on an empty stomach, and it was the only meal over which I had any control – as you can tell.

She would shut her mouth tight as I presented the spoon to her lips. This was tricky because if I didn't take care, I would spill the milk. 'Come on, Lucy.' She moved her head to one side. The spoon followed her tightly pursed mouth and she swung her head round and spilt milk all over her sweatshirt. I bet you saw that coming.

'Lucy! Look what you've done,' I shouted.

Jessica went on munching her apple – 'Oh, Luce' – and Lucy started to sob.

'Go and wipe down your school sweatshirt and come downstairs when you are feeling less grumpy. And you can't go to school unless you have had some breakfast. How about I make you a peanut butter sandwich?' Brian Redhead gave another *Today* time-check, which meant I had about six minutes to get out of the house.

Lucy knew that if she played for time she would not have to eat breakfast and, of course, she usually won because, ready or not, we had to leave the house or I would miss my train. I was flustered and in a tearing hurry. I was late. As usual. I needed to leave the house at twenty-five past eight and by now it was nearly half past. I unchained my bike and wheeled it down the road. Jessica was holding my hand. Lucy walked beside me, apparently none the worse for her tears, but with a big wet stain in the middle of her sweatshirt.

So far, so good.

Then it all began to get tricky.

We walked down the road and I called hello to the neighbour who services my car as he passed us en route to get his daily paper. Jessica had gone silent.

We crossed the road to Catherine's and I could feel Jessica holding my hand tighter and tighter. We knocked on Catherine's door and Jessica mumbled, 'I don't want you to go to work, Daddy.' She was by now squeezing my hand. Joe opened the door and rushed upstairs after a quick 'Hi'. He was busy working on an invention. I now dragged Jessica into the kitchen, where Catherine was feeding yoghurt to baby Leila, whose mouth was open like fledgling. I so wished Lucy would exhibit a similar attitude to her food.

'Sit yourselves down, girls. I shan't be a minute. Joe!' she shouted. 'Time for school! He is making a trap to catch the hedgehog who lives at the bottom of the garden. He wants it for a pet. Fleas and all. He's bonkers, isn't he, girls?'

'Can I have some toast please, Catherine?' said Lucy, as if the breakfast episode had never happened.

'Help yourself. Plastic bread or brown bread?'

'Plastic bread please.'

'There's some white already in the toaster. Don't let your dad see!'

'We had a row over Rice Krispies,' I said lamely, as I tried to unwrap Jessica's clenched fingers from my hand.

'I don't want you to go, Daddy!' she mumbled, not wanting anyone to notice.

'Come now, Jessica,' said Catherine who had clocked it all. 'Daddy has to go to work and we have to go to school. Joe can't wait for science lesson today. Apparently, Mr Standish is going to do some experiments. Do you remember last time he set the desk on fire?' The moment I unravelled Jessica's fingers, she wrapped herself round my legs. 'Daddy, don't go to work. I don't want you to go to work!' she sobbed.

'Now, now, darling. I have to go to work. If I don't work, we can't eat. You don't want to starve, do you?'

'I don't care. I DON'T WANT YOU TO GO!'

Lucy was busy spreading Nutella on her toast. We only ever had Nutella when we were on holiday.

Catherine had come over to untangle us.

'Now, Jessica, after school I thought we could have fairy cakes, like your Mum used to bake, because today is Baking Day. I wonder if you and Luce would like to help me ice them?' As a child minder and mother of six, Catherine did industrial quantities of home baking. 'What flavour icing should we make?' And under her breath to me, 'You go,' and to the girls, 'I think chocolate, although Emily says lemon.'

'Chocolate,' muttered Jessica.

'Bye, darlings. I'll see you after supper. Be good.' I kissed Lucy – who was munching her way happily through her slice of toast – on the top of her head, and Jessica on the cheek. She looked imploringly at me through tears. 'I don't . . . want . . . Daddy . . . to . . . go.'

I ignored her, made a hasty exit, shut the door and got on my bike. I caught the train, just. I would always catch the train, just. I'm so paranoid about time, I've been setting my watch fast by five minutes for the last twenty years. I have always, always been in a rush.

By the time I was seated on the train, I was exhausted.

When I got to my office I would phone Catherine. 'She's fine, Jeremy. The moment you left, she pulled herself together, stopped crying and helped Lucy feed Leila. She chatted all the way to school as if nothing had happened. She told me all about Auntie Louise getting married and her and Lucy being bridesmaids. She's so excited. She's fine.'

I used to dread crossing the road to Catherine's, because that was always when Jessica started acting like a limpet, with me as the rock.

Back to our Sunday evening debriefing and my question about Jessica's clinginess. Catherine just said, 'I've no idea. She seems OK most of the rest of the time. Whenever I pick them up from school, she always seems bright and chirpy, never asks after you. I don't know.'

We moved on to the week ahead.

'On Monday I will bring them round to you and Linda will pick them up from school. Jessica is going to Katie's for tea. Tuesday, Wednesday and Thursday, you'll take them to school. If that's OK? Linda will pick them up, except for Thursday.'

'It's Charlotte's birthday party that day.'

'I know AND we have bought her a present AND the children have wrapped it up,' I replied smugly.

'Well remembered.'

'Suzy reminded me! I will be back late on Thursday – no later than nine, but Linda has to go at seven-thirty sharp. Will Hannah be able to babysit?'

'I'll check, but I think she has band practice until seven. If not, I'm sure Tom will do it.'

'Friday, I will take them to school, as we're seeing Dr Forrest, and I think Julia will pick them up from school and give them tea, but I'll have to check. Anyway, I'm probably working from home that day.'

'Do you want me to do some of your ironing?'

A guilty pause.

'That would be great. Thank you so much. I'm OK with washing, but ironing . . .'

'Why don't you get Linda to do it?'

'Well, she irons the girls' stuff, but . . . I'm getting better at ironing, but . . . you know how it is, what with the cleaning and cooking.'

'I've had an idea about the cleaning.'

'Do tell.' I looked around our front room despairingly. Lizzie had been not so much house proud as messaphobic, whereas me . . . well, I am a man.

'Do you know Ruth Lee?'

'No.'

'She's one of the dinner ladies at New Hinksey.' She described someone who was built like a tank, was lippy, masculine, had an opinion on everything and was very Oxford – Oxford Cowley rather than Oxford Christ Church. 'I'm sure she'd be very happy to help.'

So she arranged for Ruth to come in once or twice a week and clean the house. In fact, Catherine organized a rota of all the school dinner ladies who came and blitzed our house. It might have been lifeless, but from then on it was always clean. It also meant that the girls always got big helpings of their favourite puddings at school.

'I hope you don't mind, but I noticed the other day when I was looking for a biscuit for the girls that the top cupboard in the kitchen was, well, full of cakes . . . '

'Oh dear. I just don't know what to do with them.'

'. . . a lot of half-mouldy, uneaten cakes in tins that I threw away. I hope you don't mind.'

Catherine had rumbled me.

At least once or twice a week, usually on a Friday evening, a neighbour – generally someone I only vaguely knew – would knock on our door and thrust a cake tin into my hand and say, 'I was doing a bit of baking, so I made an extra one for you. I hope you like carrot cake. It's my gran's recipe . . .' That kind of thing. I never had the heart to say, 'I hate carrot cake,' so I would thank them profusely, promise to give them back the tin at some point and then store it in what became known as the cake cupboard, a cupboard that was usually only opened a couple of times a week, to take further deliveries.

Catherine let it be known at the school gate that the Howes were growing fat on cake and probably didn't need any more for a while, and our cake mountain disappeared.

Catherine organized me and the girls in various other discreet, subtle ways, pointing me in the right direction, supporting me, and was as reliable as a rock. In all the child-care crises, she was always there.

'Catherine?'

'Hello,' she'd say at the other end of the phone.

'Hi. Bit of a problem. Lucy has just eaten some cherries – stones and all.'

'Oh dear. What a noodle.'

'Should I go to casualty?'

'How many did she eat?'

'Six, I guess.'

'You counted them in, so count them out. If they all come out in her poo, then no harm done. I am sure Jessica will know how many she has eaten. Check with her. Nothing to worry about, honestly. Must go. Leila is screaming her head off.'

That was Catherine. The patron saint of child-rearing.

And, of course, Jessica knew exactly how many cherries her sister had eaten – 'But I only had five.'

After we'd gone through the week's appointments, Catherine would kiss me on the cheek and say, 'See you tomorrow, bright and early. I'll see myself out. You're doing OK. Honestly. The girls are fine.'

And the weekend was over.

17

As I came out of the tube and walked to my office one grey November Monday, having had a particularly difficult time with the girls, I imagined I was at the wheel of an ocean-going yacht on tempestuous seas. I had the girls huddled either side of me. The wind was a cacophony, the waves mountainous and treacherous as the boat struggled against them, and I had no certainty of a safe passage. I was scared. I was hanging on, but only just.

We had been clinging to that boat for nearly four months, and surviving wasn't now a matter of confronting crises so much as getting on with the awfulness of our bereft state. But the one huge saving grace of being at work was that although I had changed, work had not. It was a lifeline back to normality for me.

But lying ahead was a whole series of events that would take us into uncharted waters. As you know, the Howes – Jeremy, Jessica, Lucy and Lizzie – had set great store by the calendar of festivals. We now had to confront them as a family of three. It felt like a minefield ahead of me. Christmas was looming, but before that was Bonfire Night and, hard on its heels, my birthday.

Every year since we had come to Oxford, we had thrown a party for Bonfire Night. It had been fun, even though Lucy went indoors for the fireworks themselves, despite the fact that I only bought boring pretty ones without bangs. This year, though, I just couldn't face it. Neighbours had a few fireworks and jacket potatoes, but it was a pale imitation of our bonfire fest, and everyone knew it. I felt a heel.

Two weeks later it was my birthday, which I tried hard to ignore. What was there to celebrate? I have mostly blotted the day from my memory. I remember that I was recording a play for Radio 3 over in west London (Hugh Grant was playing the lead – have you heard of him? He wasn't famous then), but because I had changed jobs from running the drama on Radio 3 to looking after the drama series and serials on Radio 4, I was summoned in my lunch break to a first meeting with the controller of Radio 4 in his office in Broadcasting House at the top of Regent Street, i.e. a bit of a drag. I got there late and everyone else was waiting. I offered my apologies, then one of my colleagues, who had been fumbling over something in the corner, turned round and produced a birthday cake with candles. I was overwhelmed. Later I bought Champagne for the cast, but felt utterly hollow attempting to celebrate a day I felt was best left unmarked.

Christmas, however, was a really thorny one – the girls would never have forgiven me if I'd buried it, like I had my birthday.

My plan was simple. I would take as little time off work as was humanly possible (apart from anything else, I had taken eight weeks off in the summer, so I felt guilty about taking more), and I wouldn't stand still long enough for depression to overwhelm me. Catch me if you can.

It mapped out like this:

Christmas Eve: I was off work. We went shopping in town, saw a morning matinee of a Christmas show at the Oxford Playhouse and then dropped off huge tins of Roses chocolates to various families in the street who had saved our bacon. In the afternoon Inga-Stina Ewbank stopped by with a Norwegian gingerbread house she had baked for the children, who by now were in a wild state of excitement.

We had supper with friends and then we came home. Playing Father Christmas alone, stuffing their stockings and wrapping their presents, was a melancholy affair.

Christmas Day: our stockings were opened fiendishly early. Father Christmas had made sure that as well as all the goodies that in Christmases past Daddy had invariably bought for the stockings, there were also things that were Mummy's specialities – like new toothbrushes, flannels and knickers and vests.

We rushed downstairs to inspect the gargantuan pile of presents.

We breakfasted on Coco Pops and other assorted chocolate treats.

Jessica and Lucy, dressed in their Christmas best, then opened their presents from Daddy – the chief of which was an enormous wicker dressing-up basket which Lizzie and I had promised them.

We packed up and drove to Maka and Deda's.

The car broke down in the middle of nowhere.

I called the AA.

And arrived late and flustered for lunch.

Once lunch and the Queen's speech had been dispatched, we opened more presents – Jessica and Lucy were given the fairy ballerina outfits they so coveted.

We then drove through the dark, nursing the car, to my old bosses – Karin and David's – in Somerset. More gifts.

I finally inveigled the girls to shed their fairy ballerina outfits for bedtime and the adults played Risk. Surprisingly, David, who had been one the most successful film executives in Britain until he'd retired a couple of years earlier, conquered the world.

On Boxing Day we went kite-flying and got appallingly muddy, and then, late that afternoon, we drove to my brother's. The car broke down. Again. We called the AA. Again.

We arrived flustered. There were more presents. Then we went on to my mother's, which was a difficult call for me, as it was the first time I had been back to Sudbury since Lizzie's death. It felt like I was stepping on broken glass, and I found it hard to settle. I went for a walk by myself across the water meadow. It felt weird – I couldn't reach the emotional heights of that morning after Lizzie's death. I just felt numb and miserable.

After yet more presents and an early lunch we went to the pantomime at the theatre in Colchester where I used to be a director. In the birthdays section at the end, the dame – a mate of mine – read out, 'And a very happy birthday to Mr Jeremy Howe, who is one hundred and four and a half today.' I felt cherished. After the final curtain I took Jessica and Lucy backstage to meet the cast, which they thought was utter magic, but I felt terribly lonely standing there holding their hands while we waited to be buzzed through the stage door.

And so continued our round-England tour of friends, relatives and whoever would have us.

By the time we reached home, we practically needed a trailer to ferry the excess of presents the children had been given. I remembered the year when my uncle died in the car crash – my cousin Liz came for Christmas. She had a stack of presents nearly as high as the Christmas tree and four times bigger than the combined size of our three not inconsiderable piles. It took us ten minutes to open ours and her all morning to open hers. As well as presents from people we visited, Jessica and Lucy were also sent gifts from everyone who had ever met them, and more besides. We opened the last of them on Twelfth Night and finished the Christmas chocolates sometime near Good Friday. They were given so many Advent calendars, I could have opened a shop. All the ones with chocolate, I threw away. To their complete outrage.

Easter, by contrast, was easy to manage – and fantastic.

Lucy's godfather, Eoin, whisked us away to spend the holiday in the south of Spain with two friends of his, Willy and Alison, who had a house overlooking a huge, empty beach on the Atlantic. A succession of their friends dropped by and spoilt us all rotten, Alison mothered the girls, I relaxed properly for the first time since Lizzie died and we gorged on more chocolate.

It kind of set the pattern for our future holidays.

I have always enjoyed holidays, and I got good at them as a single parent, on my own terms – i.e. never a dull moment, 300 guidebooks per interesting town, lots of excursions and not very much lazing around the pool or sunbathing. We always took them with another family (something we had never done before Lizzie's death), never just the three of us: mostly with Clive (who had taken us to Donegal) and his wife Elaine, but over the next three years we went away with half a dozen other families, as well as with assorted friends.

I am not sure I could have borne taking the girls away by myself. I would have felt so lonely and as if I was play-acting at being a family. They always enjoyed the company of other children and having a surrogate mum on hand who did all the mumsy kind of things that I was so crap at. I enjoyed it too. Having a mother on tap 24/7 who knew how to do and say the things that just didn't come naturally to me was lovely – for me as much as for the girls. As was the company, especially in the evenings, which for a single parent can seem like a vast desert of time to kill. Somehow, too, with two families together, the broken-backedness of us Howes didn't stand out – I don't mean in public (I really didn't care about that), but to me. Holidays were a way of creating some kind of family normality in my own head. And, although I was desperately hard up, we took lots of them. Basically, if someone was kind enough to even vaguely suggest, 'Would you think of coming on holiday with us?' it was firmed up within minutes. As any working mother knows, trying to stitch together a line through the six-week school summer break is like trying to solve the most fiendish equation, and holidays away helped fill those long weeks when friendship groups at home disappeared.

This meant we had gluts of summer vacations. The year after Lizzie's death, after a week in the Dordogne with Clive and Elaine, we arrived back late on Saturday night only to drive to Bath first thing on Sunday morning for the girls to go on holiday with Maka and Deda in Devon. A couple of years later, we had two and a half weeks in Greece booked, and then Clive asked me if we would like to share a villa with them in the South of France for a week just a fortnight later. Unhesitatingly, I said yes. I know it sounds ridiculous, but they were offers I felt I couldn't refuse in case they were never made again. I just closed my eyes to the state of my bank account and disregarded the amount of leave I was taking from the BBC and even the looks on other people's faces – 'Another holiday?' someone said disapprovingly. We just took them, grinned and bore the disgrace of being self-indulgent hedonists.

On holiday I felt alive. I was able to relax and really enjoy the company of Jessica and Lucy. I felt none of these things at home, if I am honest. I was in a permanent state of anxiety.

However, one particular holiday was not a success. Karin and David invited me out for a long weekend to Norway, where Karin was working. The plan was that I would arrive on Thursday after work, potter around Oslo by myself on the Friday, David would arrive on Friday evening and on Saturday through to Monday we would stay up in the mountains and then I would fly home on Tuesday. It was to be just me, without the girls – 'To give you a break,' they said. They were just about the nicest people I ever worked for, they were amongst my best friends and I knew them incredibly well. I was so looking forward to it and I had a terrible time, even though Karin and David were excellent company and generous to a fault. I am not sure Norway itself helped – going alone to the Edvard Munch Museum is not a guaranteed way to raise the spirits, and the sheer scale and emptiness of the mountain country caught me by surprise.

The hotel we stayed in overlooked a beautiful lake, with an island in the middle which we rowed out to, and there were epic views of the mountains beyond. I climbed to the crest of the hill across the lake from the hotel and there below me was another equally beautiful lake with an island and endless views of mountains receding into infinity. At noon a raven flew over the lake. It cawed. That was the only sign of life all day. The emptiness of the landscape was overwhelming enough, but the real problem was that I missed the children. Not because I missed their company so much, but because I realized that without them I was nothing. Just a lonely middle-aged man killing time in a beautiful place. I couldn't get back to them quickly enough.

But you know what children are like. You arrive home and they affect not to notice you have been away. After ten minutes of being quite nice, they start to squabble. They sort of like the presents you agonized over choosing for them and they are not the slightest, teeniest bit interested in hearing about where you have been and what you have done.

'That's nice, Daddy,' said Jessica, looking the other way and sighing. 'I am trying to watch *Pingu* and it's getting to the good bit.'

And I loved them for it.

After our Easter in Spain, we were faced with the tricky last furlong of the calendar – Lucy's birthday in May, Jessica's in early June and Lizzie's at the end of the month, topped off by the anniversary of her death a month later in July.

Lizzie and I had promised Lucy that she could have her next birthday party at the farm where Jessica had had hers. I booked it with a heavy heart. Returning would bring back such painful memories.

I needn't have worried. Lucy and her friends loved it, and Lucy loved the fact that it was exactly the same as Jessica's party last year – 'Only better, Daddy. Much better!'

A couple of days later we celebrated her proper birthday and continued the tradition Lizzie and I had started of the girls bringing up all the presents and opening them on my bed before breakfast, with a present for both girls of a bag of sweets and goodies.

For Jessica's birthday, my brother and I drove ten children up to Cadbury World. The triumph of this particular trip was that we brought back all ten, stuffed with freebie chocolate, without one of them being sick.

I had somehow managed to establish a new fun regime for birthdays, and by making them big treats and spoiling my two rotten, I had dispelled the aura of sadness that surrounded them.

I was determined to keep the sadness at bay on Lizzie's birthday too. By and large, I ignored Mother's Day. And always have ever since. But not Lizzie's birthday. That first year I bought a tiny cake with one candle and a present for the house. And that's what we've done ever since. For many years we bought Harry Potter for her birthday (JK Rowling seemed to publish annually just for us). It's our Mother's Day.

The anniversary of her death is a different matter. For one thing, I can never remember when it is exactly, so it creeps up on me and ambushes me. And then I go into an awful depression. It numbs me. I get migraines. I just want the day to be obliterated. And it never is. But the first anniversary of her death was especially awful – it coincided with the week of the trial.

18

Robin Pask had been arrested and charged within hours of the incident. There was no doubt that he had killed Lizzie.

It took nearly four years to bring him to justice.

Justice is a very important part of healing, something I had never before realized. If Pask had been found not guilty, I know deep down that I would have brought him to justice myself, and I would not have been accountable for my actions. It was an ugly feeling, a feeling that I was uneasy about, a kind of primal urge, mostly involving a double-barrelled shotgun.

Healing involves being able to travel cleanly in a straight line and whenever I began thinking about the man who was responsible for Lizzie's death, my thoughts became jagged and violent. I became angry and irrational. I spent a lot of time trying to blot him out of my life. I wanted to get back to an image of Lizzie that didn't involve her violent death, which shrouded my happy memories with a curtain of pain. Like Jessica and Lucy, I wanted the wound to be clean.

Pask's impending trial was getting in the way of that process.

And then there were the police to contend with.

The two things are fused together in my head.

My relationship with the police hadn't really recovered from my experiences at York Police Station. I was wary of them. Whenever they called me, I could feel my heart rate go up.

One Thursday morning, in the spring of 1993, they phoned me at the office. How did they get my number? I guess they were detectives and that's what detectives do.

'Mr Howe, something new has come up and we wondered if we could see you.'

'Why can't you just tell me now?'

'No. It's best done in person.'

'OK. When?'

'Tomorrow?'

'OK.'

'We would like to meet you at your home in Oxford.'

'But I'm at work tomorrow. Why don't you come to the office?' I was anxious. I reasoned that they wouldn't dare do anything untoward on BBC premises.

'How about Saturday?'

'Well, I am busy,' I lied. I had no plans for the weekend. 'Why don't you come to the office tomorrow?'

'You name a time on Saturday and we will be there. In Oxford.'

'Well, it's really not convenient.'

'Any time. Early is fine.'

I calculated that it was about a three-hour drive from York. I wanted to make it as inconvenient for them as

I could without seeming unreasonable. I did not want the police in my house.

'Can you be there by nine?'

'No problem.'

Damn.

'You might have to wait outside. I've got to do the week's shopping first thing.'

'Fine.'

'How will I know it's you?'

'You'll know who we are, don't worry.'

'And can you tell me what this is all about?'

'We will tell you on Saturday. Goodbye, Mr Howe. And thank you.'

I was convinced they were going to arrest me. Irrational, I know, but I felt that the police had tried to snare me once before. I phoned my sister and told her about what was happening and how worried I was. Much to her husband's annoyance, she pandered to her brother's paranoia and agreed to be in Oxford the next morning. I wanted a witness and somebody to look after the children if I was carted away.

I woke the girls up especially early on the Saturday morning and they rather grumpily came with me to Sainsbury's before eight o'clock. Philippa was due to arrive at nine, to coincide with the police. I bought enough provisions to withstand a siege – in case I had to go away. I even bought the police officers a cake each: how could they arrest me if I'd bought them a cake?

As we drove down our street, laden with shopping, we saw a red Ford Sierra with an enormous aerial on the roof. It had to be either the Dukes of Hazzard or the police. As I parked the car and the children helped me unload the entire stock of Sainsbury's, two burly guys got out of the Sierra and started helping with the shopping. In their leather bomber jackets, they were like a parody of extras from *The Bill*. They had been right, though – I did know who they were.

We went in, greeted my sister, who had arrived as we had, and I made them coffee. As I unpacked the shopping, they prowled around the kitchen and chatted to me.

I remember one of them picking up one of the only photographs we have of the four of us. It was taken in the States, it was boiling hot, we were all wearing shorts.

'I can tell this is a holiday snap,' one of them said.

'How?' I said

'I am a detective.' He grinned.

You probably won't believe this, but that is the only scrap of conversation I can remember. Nor can my sister recall what they talked about. If I were to write out the whole scene for you, it would be an entirely fictitious rip-off of *The Wire*. I just cannot remember what happened, and I have no idea why they came or what they came to tell me. It felt like it was a PR exercise, to show how caring the police can be.

Interestingly, I wrote a piece for the *Sunday Times* a few years later and used this story as the centrepiece of the article – and the North Yorkshire Police threatened legal action against me.

They stayed about half an hour and then went. They didn't even eat the cakes I'd bought. Once they had gone, I felt sick.

Their visit ranks as one of the worst experiences in a whole ghastly series of worst experiences. Which perhaps says more about my state of mind in the spring of 1993 than anything about the way the police behaved.

One of the things gnawing away at me was that I wanted Lizzie's things back from the police. I could understand that some of them might be required as evidence against Pask, but not her lecture notes, her wedding ring, the watch I had given her the Christmas before last, her knick-knacks, etc. Most of all, I wanted back the lovely blue and white kitten mug the girls had given her for her birthday four weeks before her death and which she – loving mum that she was – had made a point of taking with her to York. I thought these things might help me get her back somehow, and surely they were of no use in the case?

'But we require all of it for evidence and we can't return anything until after the trial, Mr Howe.'

'When will that be?'

'Well, the wheels of justice move slowly, sir. It could be anything up to a year.'

'I see.'

Pause.

'But I want everything returned.'

'Sorry, Mr Howe, but I'm afraid we will destroy most of your late wife's effects.'

'You can't do that! I want them back. They are precious. Why?'

'Well, sir, a lot of her things are – how can I put this nicely, Mr Howe? – are covered in her blood. They would be a health risk. We will have to incinerate them, sir.'

'I see. But can't I at least see them to find out what is important and what is not?'

'No, sir. It is evidence.'

'Even if I come up to York?' This was a big step for me – York was not a place I much wanted to visit.

'You cannot tamper with evidence that we might require to use in the trial. I'm sure you understand, sir.'

'You see, I don't know what is there, what will be of value. You know, as mementos, keepsakes . . . Is there at least an inventory of her things I could see?'

'I will certainly look into it, sir.'

I felt so far away from Lizzie. The loss of her was a constant ache in my stomach, a tightening in my chest.

To my surprise, a week or two later, an inventory arrived in the post. It was vague and meaningless – 'papers', 'sundry items', 'clothes, some bloodstained' etc., etc. I wanted a list that gave me a sense of what she had left behind. This list meant nothing. Neither could it have meant much to the prosecution team trying to use it as evidence in a trial. What was particularly painful was that I had such a strong image of all Lizzie's stuff laid out in clear plastic bags on a table in a corridor in York Police Station the day after her death – so close then and now utterly un-reachable. I felt terrible. Thwarted. Betrayed.

I phoned them. It took for ever to get through. About half a dozen phone calls later I got to speak to the right person. We wrangled and reached a compromise, and he agreed to send down a few of the more precious things.

A couple of weeks later I picked up a phone message saying that a package had arrived at Oxford Police Station and would I collect it.

I went down there and waited at the lost-property hatch. The boy in front of me was collecting his stolen bike they had recovered. He looked so pleased to have got it back. I waited with trepidation. I signed for the package. A box? An envelope full of papers? They handed over a small jiffy bag. I was crestfallen. I thanked them and walked quickly out of the police station. Once outside, I tore open the envelope: Lizzie's wedding ring and her watch in a small plastic bag. The leather strap was stained dark in places with her blood. I was both elated and terribly cast down – so much and so little. Was it Christmas or Ash Wednes-day? I took off my watch and replaced it with hers. I wore the watch until it gave up the ghost a year later. It made me feel just a little bit closer to Lizzie. It narrowed the chasm separating us by a few inches, but the wedding ring was a different matter. In truth, I didn't know what to do with it. On Lizzie's finger it had meant so much, but in my hand it was just a cheap band of gold from H. Samuel. I wondered if I should wear it round my neck on a chain, but in the end I just squirrelled it away.

Months later a random package of Lizzie's papers arrived in the post. It included the Stevie Smith lecture she was due to deliver on the evening of her death. I couldn't read it. I have never been able to read it. Just thinking about it fills me with dread. Mind you, reading anything academic fills me with dread. I blagged my way to a very respectable degree from a world-class university, but I am no scholar. These lecture notes, though, are something different. They are bloodstained. It could just be from a nose bleed or from a cut finger, but I know it is not. I can imagine them on her desk in her room in York, and then my mind shuts down. I just can't go there.

Trying to imagine what came next for Lizzie was impossible, but the reality of her trial was still hanging over me. And of course it was the trial that I was really dreading.

Regina vs Pask.

First, just days after Lizzie's death, Pask appeared at a magistrate's court, where he was charged and was denied bail. It was a news story. It was painful. But it was a blip.

Then he was referred to the High Court. Another news story. He entered a plea of not guilty of murder, but guilty of manslaughter with diminished responsibility. I got accustomed to the glacial progress the case was making through the legal system, about which I realized I knew absolutely nothing.

The trial itself would not take place for almost a year. Why? I learned from the police that Pask was in the hospital wing of a prison in Hull, awaiting psychological reports (why didn't they just interview him straightaway?), that there was a shortage of High Court judges (I wrote to the Lord Chancellor asking why there weren't more), and then that the trial slated for May had been put back while the defence prepared their case. What case? Although he never admitted to murdering Lizzie, he did admit to being the only person in the room when she died. How many angels can you get dancing on the head of a pin?

It made us all feel anxious. One Friday morning after Christmas, the post arrived bearing a letter informing me that the trial had been delayed. Maka was staying with us, as she often did. Because I was working at home that day, I took the children to school. Lucy had been a real pain at breakfast and Jessica had been painfully clingy at the school gate.

As I walked back through the park, on that grey day, pregnant with rain, with the line of pines that straddled the park silhouetted against the lowering sky, I thought of Pask and was overcome with grief and self-pity. I started sobbing uncontrollably. I stood in the empty park and shouted out, 'You cunt! You fucking cunt! I hate you! You bastard! Look what you have done to us! I HATE YOU!'

It was a bit OTT, I know, and even as I stood there I was aware that I was acting like a character in an Ingmar Bergman film. But I was bereft. Utterly bereft.

When I arrived home, still miserable, Maka got up from doing her crossword. She too had been fretting over the news of the trial. We hugged.

'I am so sorry. Poor Lizzie. Poor, poor Lizzie. That wretched bloody man.'

I pulled myself together and wiped my nose. I cried my way through so many handkerchiefs that year. As I write this, I can recall the feeling of sodden handkerchiefs in my pocket.

'I am going to have a stiff whisky. Will you join me?' she asked.

It was ten past nine in the morning and the sun was no-where near the yard arm. I opted for a cup of decaff coffee and a Penguin biscuit, and even that felt a bit decadent just after breakfast. I would never dull the pain with alcohol, I wanted to try to keep control. But that was Maka's prob-lem – she tried to drink away her sorrows, but drink never flushed them away.

Not long after the letter about the delay to the trial, I received a notice of summons from the High Court. It said that because I had given evidence in the case, I might be called upon to give evidence at the trial of Regina vs Pask, and failure to do so might result in prosecution. Very help-fully attached to the summons was a line drawing of what a court looks like, from which it was all too clear that when I gave evidence I would be standing right next to the man who had killed my wife. I felt nauseous. I phoned the police.

'It's a form letter, sir, and you shouldn't have been sent

it. You will not be required to give evidence or to attend the trial. We apologize.'

It was an endurance test, a test during which I learnt that the victim and the victim's relatives (i.e. me) had no place in the criminal justice system. I was a nuisance.

A new date was set for the trial.

It was the anniversary of Lizzie's death.

The police wanted to know if I would attend.

'What provision is made for the victim's family?'

'Well, sir, you sit in the public gallery.'

'Do we have special seating?'

'Well, no, sir, seating is on a first come, first served basis, sir.'

'So I might not even get in.'

'That's a possibility, sir.'

'And I might be sitting next to *his* family?'

'That too is a possibility, sir.'

I had visions of a Hogarthian court house with me trapped beside the Pask family amidst the rabble.

'Also, I should warn you that the press will be on the lookout for you.'

The prosecution barrister got in touch. He wondered if we might meet up the week before the trial.

One evening that week I left work early and met him in a suitably Dickensian wine bar opposite the Royal Courts of Justice. A slightly overweight Yorkshireman, dressed in a very expensive suit, he exuded both the good life and immense capability. I liked him.

'I don't know what your plans are, but I would strongly advise that you don't come to the trial.'

'I think I have already made up my mind. As I see it, I have a lot to lose from going and nothing to gain.'

'Sensible chap. You see, I think you might be expecting the truth to emerge in a trial, and you'll get nothing like it. It's a game between me and the defence barrister. All we are trying to do is score points. I will do anything to get a result, and so will he. And in that situation, I'm afraid, the truth is invariably a victim.'

He outlined how he was planning to proceed in the trial. He was the first person in nearly a year who sat me down and explained how the justice system works and talked to me like an equal. I left the bar feeling immensely grateful – because out of the fog of misinformation, partial truths, of jargon that hid plain-speaking, here was a man who told me what was what and had taken the time to tell me directly.

The week of the trial was high summer at its hottest. It was an appalling week, almost unendurable – I now understand why trials are so called: it was like waiting for an operation to remove my heart. The pressure made me feel as if I were being shaken until I broke, and all the while I tried to conduct myself as if everything was normal. I took meetings at work, I read scripts, I smiled on the way to school, I shared in the girls' excitement about their imminent summer holidays. But it was a mask.

The police had agreed to keep me informed of the trial's

progress, my wonderful personnel officer arranged a rota of friends and colleagues to take me out to lunch every day and Lizzie's sister Louise travelled north to Leeds Crown Court with her new husband to witness proceedings.

On day one, Pask entered a plea of not guilty.

'But he killed her,' I told the police on the phone when they reported back.

'Yes, but he is hoping to get convicted of manslaughter with diminished responsibility.'

'What does that mean?'

'That he is admitting he is insane.'

'What's the difference between manslaughter and murder?'

'Well, it's an odd one, Mr Howe. If it was murder he would get a life sentence and serve fourteen or so years in prison, but with diminished responsibility he will be sent to a prison hospital and probably remain there for life.'

'Why would he choose to do that?'

'My guess, Mr Howe, is that he can't face up to his crime. He would rather hide behind a verdict of insanity than face up to the murder of your late wife. If you ask me, he is a murderer, plain and simple.'

Louise phoned me to tell me that in court Pask looked like a worm. 'God, Jeremy, I am so glad you didn't come here. There are hordes of press photographers waiting for you on the steps of the court, all with photographs of you so they can identify you.'

Meanwhile, BBC Leeds did a TV interview with me in

the Langham Hotel opposite my office. It made me feel special – well, kind of special. I mean, they booked a posh room in a posh hotel just to interview me.

On day two, Pask's sister and his mother gave evidence *against* him.

'Mr Howe, in my experience, murder trials rarely go to plan, and with that evidence I can't see the trial lasting the week. Something strange is going to happen, mark my words, Mr Howe.'

On day three, all the evidence about what Pask actually did to Lizzie came out in court. What he did to her after she was dead was unspeakable.

I was sitting in my office just before lunch the next day, discussing a dramatization of Daphne du Maurier's *The Scapegoat* with a producer, when my phone rang. It was the police.

'Mr Howe, the trial has collapsed.'

'What!?'

The producer made signs to me and slunk out of my office.

'Pask collapsed in court and the trial has been adjourned while doctors make an assessment of his health.'

'Till when?'

'Indefinitely.'

'So what will happen?'

'I don't even know if the case will come to court again. The judge instructed that Pask should be submitted for psychiatric testing to establish his suitability to stand trial.'

I felt cheated. Sick. Exhausted. I wanted to lie down, to curl up and go to sleep.

Louise called me on a pay phone from the court lobby.

'I told you he was a worm. He was being led from the court and deliberately tripped over a chair. I saw it. He is faking it. He is scared. The bastard.'

I made my apologies to my secretary and went home. I was bunking off. But I was shattered. The story was in the early edition of the *London Evening Standard* I bought for the train journey. It was on the news on telly.

By the time I got home it was early evening, sultry and overcast. I was like a cat on hot bricks. I didn't know what to do with myself. I don't think I had ever felt so alone in my life. A friend of Lizzie's from university came round to see how I was and we went for a walk round the park at the end of our street. I was so obviously distraught. I remember her giving me a hug. I can still feel the warmth of her body pressed to mine. It was such a familiar feeling, such a lost feeling. I so wanted Lizzie back, and I don't think I ever felt further from her in my life.

That weekend, we marked the anniversary of Lizzie's death by having a short service in the pouring rain to bless the gravestone in the cemetery above Bath. I had so fretted over it: what kind of stone, what shape, what inscription? I wanted everything to be as simple as possible – just as Lizzie was a simple and straightforward person, so her grave had to be. It was in plain Bath stone, with a curving top, a simple line etched all the way round the edge and the inscription 'My heart's best treasure'. Wordsworth again. I felt I had done the right thing by her.

From then on, Lucy and I would visit the grave every Mother's Day with a bunch of daffodils. Jessica has never been since that day.

Nearly three years later, Robin Pask was brought to a retrial. He entered a plea of guilty to manslaughter with diminished responsibility and was sentenced to detention at Her Majesty's pleasure in a prison hospital. The trial lasted half a day. 'Life means life, Mr Howe. And Ashworth isn't a pleasant place. I am just so sorry it has taken so long.' A few papers gave the story a paragraph. I felt a bit cheated, but mightily relieved. Justice had been served. End of story.

Nearly.

The day after the verdict was announced I phoned York Police Station to enquire about getting Lizzie's things back and was told I needed to speak to the duty sergeant.

'Of course we will send them, Mr Howe, once we have received a cheque for seven pounds and thirty pence to cover postage and packing.'

'I can't believe you are saying this to me.'

'It's only the rules. I abide by the rules. Please make it payable to North Yorkshire Constabulary, Mr Howe, and then we will send them.'

'How about if I charge you seven pounds thirty for the use of my wife's things for four years? Then we are quits.'

'Don't get sarcastic with me, Mr Howe.'

'Sorry.'

Pause.

'I will send the cheque.'

I was in the office. I put down the phone. 'I can't believe what I have just been told.'

My PA, who had heard the conversation, was appalled. 'Why don't you phone the Chief Constable?'

'Yes. I might,' I said uncertainly.

'Go on. Do it now, while you are still angry.'

So I did and, amazingly, I got through. He heard me out, apologized and said the parcel would be sent. Right away. Forget about the cheque.

When it arrived – a big brown paper parcel – it sat threateningly in the kitchen like an unexploded bomb. I couldn't touch it.

It was the most toxic parcel I have ever received.

After several days of it sitting there untouched, I sat down with Louise and opened it. There was my briefcase (JP Howe, Form 5A), Lizzie's wallet, the birthday mug with the kitten, her ID cards, her return rail ticket to Oxford, a taxi receipt, her university notes, lists scrawled on scraps of paper in her large, hurried, restless handwriting, the pictures of the girls she took away with her, her biros, a couple of dresses, some moisturizer, crumpled-up tissues, etc., etc. The detritus of the living, only old, like exhibits in a museum.

For a second I got Lizzie back, my Lizzie, and then she vanished.

It was unbelievably painful. But there was some closure, as they say.

Tactfully, Louise put the case away from sight. I have no idea where it is.

19

The original trial finished the day before the girls broke up, the day that Linda handed in her notice.

I can only imagine that the strain of dealing with a family in meltdown must have been awful. Of course, it just felt normal to me, but for a twenty-year-old trying to look after two emotionally fragile girls, a father who wasn't coping and a whole street of well-meaning neighbours watching her every step, a year was enough and she capitulated. I don't think we ever heard from her again.

I was both relieved – it had never really worked – and in a blind panic: the whole edifice of childcare had collapsed.

I was back at square one. A year on from Lizzie's death and I was in bits on account of the trial. I had no clear idea how I was going to get through the holidays, but I knew that this year there was no way I could take six weeks off work.

'I know just the person you need.' The wonderfully capable woman who ran the nanny agency and who had given me hope a year ago remembered me when I phoned her, and she came up trumps. She drew up a list of people for me to see, we met them, Lucy didn't hit any of them, and we appointed Annette, loud, bottle-blonde (I wonder where Jessica now gets her hair colouring from?), bubbly and immensely likeable. Her previous job had been as a karaoke singer in Tenerife. She was almost as bad a cook as me, but she loved the children, the children loved her and she was a brilliant nanny. And, astonishingly, she was free to start almost right away.

'I thought you might get on with Annette,' said the nanny agency lady with a smile, and we did, as did the whole neighbourhood. Annette was perhaps more Eliza Doolittle than PL Travers, but Mary Poppins comes in many different guises. And this Poppins came bursting into our lives in full Dolby surround sound and Technicolor.

She made the children prize-winning costumes for fancy dress parties, she played singing games, made them toffee apples with dolly mixtures stuck in them for a fireworks party and put their hair up in every shape and form of plait imaginable. She read them stories, got them fixated on TV game shows, got them to tidy up, to brush their teeth, comb their hair, change their knickers – and made it all feel like fun. And she was strict to boot:

'Why is Jessica in her pyjamas at the table?' I said one evening when I got home from work.

'Daddy, Annette won't let me get down until I eat all of this up,' she sulked.

'Quite right.'

'But it's horrible. I hate chicken soup. Look it's all cabbage.'

She slopped bits of lukewarm cabbagey gruel off her spoon. She had a point.

'Lucy ate all hers up.'

'No she didn't. She went to Esther's for tea. It's not fair. I want a cuddle.'

'You'll get a cuddle when you eat three more mouthfuls.'

'Hmph. I hate you too.'

She also introduced the girls to the wonders of Rodgers and Hammerstein, or more particularly *The Sound of Music* (I think you'll find it is the story where the nanny gets the widowed dad), which they have now seen a zillion and one times and I have never watched in its entirety. On the grounds that it might have been a dangerous influence on me.

The highpoint of my children's lives was almost certainly watching Annette appear on *The Crystal Maze* on telly. Every friend Jessica and Lucy have ever had has been sat down in front of the television and made to watch the tape of it, while being subjected to an extra commentary from the girls.

For the year Annette was with us, it seemed that the sun was always shining.

I often wondered if I was the world's worst mum.

I wasn't. But sometimes it felt like a pretty near-run thing.

Love, warmth, tenderness, creating a home that is stable

and caring, giving your children the best possible start in life. I guess these are the key attributes of being a good parent. I think that, on the whole, I was pretty good at supplying these to Jessica and Lucy in the broader sense. But being a good mum is also about the detail. Clean clothes, brushed hair, good food, smart trainers that fit, and so on and so forth. What are all those skills that make women so effortlessly good at child-rearing? What qualities would I need to develop to enable me to become a domestic goddess?

Patience. No. I found it very hard to help them to learn to read or ride a bicycle for hours on end. It was a kind of act of superhuman will. I would far rather go and read the *Guardian.*

Clean clothes and all those kinds of things? Well, I was OK at that sporadically, but being systematic and rigorous was always a bit of an issue. Once a month or so I could be a very enthusiastic tidier-upper or washer, but doing it on a daily basis seemed to be beyond me.

I learnt to put the girls' hair into ponytails and, once in a blue moon, I had the patience to put them into bunches, but plaits were a grade above me.

I would brush their hair, but not without them yelping. I wasn't very patient at teasing out the tangles, so they learnt to brush their own and each other's hair. I even suggested they got their hair cut short, but it was a suggestion that was treated with scorn. In fact, I never once managed to get their hair cut. The hair-cut fairy must have done that, because they always looked presentable.

I never really mastered the nit comb and lived in perpetual fear of finding a head louse, because I didn't really know how to go about getting rid of it. They probably had nits for years, but I failed to notice.

I also lived in fear of their first periods.

I do remember Jessica, aged six, trying to explain the facts of life to Lucy, aged four, and deciding now was not the time to intervene. But when was? I did try with Jessica once, but she said, 'I know all that, Daddy. Maka told me.'

I learnt to have pockets full of pots of Sudocrem, elastoplasts, tissues and hair scrunchies, but rarely the right thing at the right time.

I got pretty good at packing swimming costumes and towels, but never remembered the comb. However, on one occasion I did forget to pack towels and the girls had to walk around the outside of the pool until they dried off.

Also, I never seemed to be able to pack spare clothes. I could get the girls out the door efficiently, but never with the right clothes for the weather, and even if I packed a spare pair of everything, my two would conspire to soak, muddy, rip or render useless at least one item of clothing I had failed to think of. I therefore have a suspiciously large number of photographs of the girls looking fetching wearing something of mine on our outings.

And the house was a place full of unfamiliar domestic terror, of machines that never seemed to work for me, of piles of papers and washing that I never seemed to be able to clear, of hooks hung with too many coats, drawers stuffed with too many clothes, none of which fitted, and a garden that was hopelessly rampant. I used to dread the spring when the grass started growing.

I never quite mastered the art of sorting washing. I was pretty good at separating whites from coloureds (getting it wrong was too dangerous – having once been scolded by Jessica for giving her pinky-grey underwear, I learnt my lesson), but I invariably failed to spot those bastard tissues lodged in pockets that ruin any wash and I always had a well-rinsed cheque book. Actually pushing those washing machine buttons to set the machine in progress has a nerve-wracking finality about it that I still find daunting. I never knew whose knickers were whose, if a sock was a part of a pair or a single one. It would take me for ever to sort out their drawers, whereas the girls were demon sorters and seemed to know where everything should be kept.

Watching me iron was a pitiful sight; ironing was best left to others.

In the winter my children always had chapped hands, because the art of keeping gloves in pairs was to me an insoluble mystery.

However, they learnt how to throw good, firm snow-balls, were excellent at treasure hunts, were utterly fearless about the scariest fairground rides, tree-climbing was second nature to them and they became ferocious card players who played to win – things I can be very proud of. Mind you, despite my best endeavours, they were pretty crap at football.

If it had been down to me, not one piece of their clothing would have had a name tape, not so much because I couldn't sew, but because threading a needle was, well, like getting a camel through its eye. However, name tapes would mysteriously appear on their clothes every time their grandmothers came to stay. To be honest, I was resigned to sourcing most of their clothes not from their wardrobe but from the school lost-property basket, which I got to know very well.

Shopping was never very systematic and always very fast. I like the idea of shopping, but only for one thing at a time. I was the guy you would see sitting in Tammy Girl reading *Private Eye*. Foodwise, it was feast or famine, so that by Friday we would be short of an evening meal but had enough toilet rolls to last the siege of Leningrad, and there were always five boxes of chicken nuggets frozen solid into the freezer compartment of the fridge, which could be prised out only after a twenty-minute attack with a sharp knife and a saw.

By now you are with acquainted with my culinary philosophy – that cooking is hell. When I told Jessica I was writing this book, she said, 'So, Daddy, you are going to write a book about how you cooked us fish fingers every day for four years.' If it came out of a packet, I could cook it, although not well; otherwise, what I served up was probably not worth eating, not so much because it tasted awful, but because I was in such an advanced state of stress that no one could bear to sit at the table with me. I have never knowingly roasted a chicken – it is way beyond my powers of time co-ordination. Two bubbling pans I can cope with, but combine them with having to watch an oven and it is just too much. In fact, I don't trust ovens generally. They can be added to the long list of household appliances of which I am wary (power drills, lawn mowers, washing machines, ironing boards, mops, freezer cabinets, bread bins, etc., etc.). At least with a grill you know where you are.

I baked a cake once. It redefined the word 'rock' as applied to cakes. 'Daddy,' Jessica said after I had slaved at it all one Saturday afternoon, 'why didn't you just buy one from the shop?'

I still don't understand why the girls refused to eat the meat pie I served up with a top so blackened it looked like I had covered it in boot polish. Nothing wrong with a bit of vigorous scraping, my grandmother would have said. The bin was surrounded by burnt breadcrumbs most days.

Waste management was also a bit of an issue. I've never been convinced that bins need frequent emptying – I find the forceful use of a foot on top of the rubbish creates plenty of space.

And why was the vacuum cleaner always blocked? Why were the bags for our particular model only available from a shop that closed at weekends, and why, once I had taken annual leave to purchase them, did I instantly mislay them? In fact, most of my housekeeping time was spent looking for things I had lost.

Food waste was worse. Before I could fill the fridge with the week's shopping, I needed to empty it of all the fresh pasta hardened to a crisp, the stray fossilized bacon rasher, the unopened curdled milk and eye-sprouting potatoes. And the bread bin seemed to need washing weekly to get rid of the aroma of mould.

I just wasn't very effective at throwing things away. But even I can see that it was perhaps unnecessary to move house in 1994 with a jar of pasta sauce with a sell-by date of 1993 on its lid.

For ages we drove around with a festering cooked chicken in the car boot because I couldn't find it (stuck in a wellington boot, I seem to recall, although Jessica disputes this), but we kind of got used to the smell. Car-boot management was a problem too. There were always seven wellington boots in there, only three of which fitted anyone. And why was the glove compartment always full of dried-out wet wipes, coagulated mints and slightly sticky lolly sticks?

In one way I was supremely feminine – if something went wrong with the car, or a machine of any description, I called a man to help me, as in: 'Julia, I've got a problem. Any chance of Ollie coming over to help me?'

Mess makes me quite short-tempered. I was short-tempered for about four years.

In four years, the children almost never had a day off school, not because they weren't sickly, but because I just pretended not to notice or gave them Calpol. They never complained. Well, not to me.

I don't think anyone ever received a birthday card on time, neither was any bill paid on arrival. I needed a red bill and a threatening letter before I would start the panicked search for my cheque book.

And the children were always hopelessly in arrears with their pocket money, so there would be endless bargaining, usually in the toy shop in Oxford on a Saturday, along the lines of: 'If I give you this eighty-seven pence,' – always in coppers – 'and you pay for the rest with the four weeks' pocket money you owe me and my pocket money for the next fortnight, then you will owe me twenty-eight pee in three Saturdays' time.' It meant that Lucy was fiendishly good at mental arithmetic. She should have done my tax return for me, which was so late and in such a state of chaos in 1993 that the Inland Revenue just said, 'Forget it.' And, of course, I was always raiding their piggy bank to pay the milk bill, so it was always full of IOUs.

I still owe Jessica the bike I promised her for her birthday one year, but as she might not read this and I have the IOU note in my desk, I am hoping she won't remember and hold me to ransom for it.

In short, nothing ever seemed to be under control and I spent most of my life worrying about the things I hadn't done, rather than actually doing them. There were some things I was good at (well, OK at) and others I was hopeless at. Would I ever master peeling cooked peppers or getting the MOT on the car done on time? Fat chance.

But, in the end, we were a happy family and a loving

one, albeit a family wearing odd socks and with holes in our jeans.

And I always got the children to the dentist for their check-ups.

I have had two anti-role models in my life – my father and my aunt. I have tried not to emulate my father's parenting, or lack of it, nor, as a single parent, have I copied my aunt. I chose to swim, she chose not to.

So, to sum up, the Jeremy Howe rules of mothering are:

Where at all possible, delegate. By profession, I was an executive producer. Execs don't actually do anything; they tell/persuade/inveigle other people to do things for them. Amazingly, some people like darning tights.

If you can't do it, don't even try. I would list baking, ironing, nit-combing, roasting and plaiting as some of the many accomplishments that I knew were way beyond me. So I never tried.

Let your children get on with it. The girls became very self-sufficient very fast. I once said to Jessica that bringing them up is the achievement I am most proud of in my life. 'Bringing you up, Daddy, was Lucy's and my proudest achievement. Mind you, I am not sure that I would allow my eight-year-old to grill toast.'

And, finally, when the house becomes too messy, move.

I wasn't the world's worst mum. I was one of the world's better mummydaddys.

*

This bit is all about sex and the single parent.

Don't be fooled into thinking you are about to read a pick-up manual or a steamy account of my sex life.

There wasn't one.

How odd to have shared a life and a bed with someone you love, to share all those intimacies and intricacies of life with someone who then disappears. Vanishes.

Which left me with an interesting challenge, particularly as I wasn't about to marry Jane from a few doors down. I was a free agent, could play the field. Well, Jessica, Lucy and I could play the field.

What I soon discovered is that single dads are not like single mums. Both are sexual outcasts, but in completely different ways.

No man will go near a single mum, for fear of entrapment, I guess, of being burdened with kids. By contrast, I was inundated by women who mercifully wanted – and maybe some needed – to hold out a hand to help me. And, boy, did I need help. I can think of a dozen or more women, some of whom I knew well, some of whom I had never really met before, who just scooped up Jessica, Lucy and me and made sure we were clothed, washed and fed. They were my lifeline. I became part of a sisterhood. They welcomed me in and I became an Honorary Mother.

But that is not the same as having a date. I wanted to be Hugh Grant in *Four Weddings and a Funeral*. Now that was a bit more tricky.

I found myself sitting on trains looking at women in a

totally new way – were they single, might they be the kind of person I could fall in love with? It was all a bit unfamiliar, quite daunting – and strangely exciting.

There was a woman who used to commute from Oxford on my train. She was about my age, Australian, gregarious, smartly turned out. I was fascinated by her and would sometimes sit close to her just so I could earwig. I discovered she caught the same tube as me, got out at Oxford Circus like me and, lo and behold, one morning she – fifty yards ahead of me – went into Broadcasting House like me! There was an in. And no, I wasn't stalking her.

But when several days elapsed and I did not see her, I felt strangely cheated. So the next time we were on the same train and the same tube, as we walked up the station steps at Oxford Circus, I summoned up the courage:

'I see you work at BH like me.'

'Hi. Yeah, I freelance for *Newsbeat* sometimes.'

'Oh, I'm in the drama department. I'm Jeremy.'

'Hi, I'm Megan.'

And as we walked up Regent Street she shook my hand, which was both weirdly formal and rather touching.

We walked in silence. I was dumbstruck.

'So you travel in from Oxford daily?' she asked.

'Every day. The eight forty-seven. Costs me a fortune.'

'I couldn't do that. I come in a couple of times a week unless I'm away on a job. I go abroad a lot. I was in Belgrade last week. I actually work for ABC. As a reporter.'

By which time we were at Broadcasting House.

'Hey, nice to meet you. See you on the train sometime.'

'Nice to meet you. Bye!'

It was the first time in fifteen years that I had introduced myself to a woman as a single man. After only two minutes' conversation I felt exhilarated. I felt like a member of the human race, like an all-conquering alpha male. I can't tell you how reckless I felt.

After that, Megan and I met on the train a number of times. She was incredibly friendly, married to a lecturer at an Oxford college, kind of knew who I was before she met me (after all, she was a journalist who sometimes worked for the BBC, where Lizzie's death had been a big issue). We became friends; she doted on Jessica and Lucy and we would go round to her house for afternoon tea. She was lovely. But she was a friend, not a romantic attachment.

A year after Lizzie's death Libby Purves asked to interview me for *Good Housekeeping*. I was trying to raise money for the Open University trust fund in Lizzie's name, so I agreed.

The interview itself was strange – Libby just appeared one morning at my front door (by arrangement, of course) and for two hours appeared to talk at me. She was very engaging and I enjoyed her company – no wonder she was a chat-show host, I thought. But I felt like I had sat mute for a couple of hours while she entertained me. I wondered if she had enough material for a paragraph, let alone a profile.

A couple of days later she faxed through her copy for the article for me to see. It was as if she had taken an X-ray photograph of me and my emotions. It was devastatingly accurate. I was unnerved.

She phoned me that evening.

'Jeremy, I just wanted to clarify one thing you said – about *The Winter's Tale*.'

'Well, the last thing Lizzie and I saw together at the theatre was this extraordinary production of it. It has haunted me ever since. It is the most moving statement about how love survives a tragedy like ours. Leontes loses Hermione. I know that it is in a fit of jealousy, that he has done her a terrible wrong by banishing her, but when he hears of her death he is inconsolable. The passage of time helps heal his wound and at the end of the play, when he is presented with a life-sized statue of Hermione, he gazes on it in love and grief 'which sixteen winters cannot blow away'. And then the statue comes to life. Hermione and Leontes have been reunited. It is the most amazing tale of enduring love, of love surviving catastrophe. And that statue coming to life is my fantasy. For me, that last scene of *The Winter's Tale* – which is magically inexplicable, so much so that Shakespeare tells us so – is what I want my life to be.'

She had asked me about remarriage. 'Of course, I have had that thought,' I told her, 'but, you see, what I desperately want is to fall in love again. With Lizzie. Again. And to have another child with her.'

She made this the basis of her closing paragraph and sent me a book that she thought might be helpful. It was.

I read *How Not To Be a Perfect Mother* and realized that I passed the How Not To test with top honours.

The article was published. My boss phoned me.

'I saw Libby's piece in *Good Housekeeping*. Very nice. She is a bright thing – she has caught you to a tee. Was it sponsored by a dating agency? I'm sure you will get several offers of marriage from it!' And he laughed and rang off.

I was very embarrassed – but he was right, of course. I might just as well have put my contact details and 'eligible and presentable middle-aged man with two adorable kids seeks kind, loving woman with a GSOH' at the bottom, to round it off neatly. It even had the most lovely photograph of the three of us. And the adorable man is doing it all for charity! What a guy!

If only they had published it on Valentine's Day.

I did get a couple of the barmiest letters from women who thought I had coped brilliantly and sounded like a very special person and would I like to share my troubles with them – with phone numbers attached – which I read with even more embarrassment. It would have been so easy to ring them. So easy! I showed them to a friend and she and I laughed and I threw them away. But secretly I was sorry I didn't get more letters.

And then, quite late one Sunday evening, came a knock at the door. It was Sam. A neighbour.

She was a bit older than me, quite attractive, resolutely single and . . . well, just a little bit intense. And very 'alternative', as in I am sure she ate macrobiotic rice and burnt joss sticks. Alternative is a word that always makes me go into spasm. So a complete match then.

After Lizzie's death Sam always stopped to pass the time of day. She would also call by occasionally. She was desperate to alleviate my suffering with reiki. I was desperate not to alleviate my suffering with reiki. But there she stood on my doorstep.

'Hi, Jeremy. Sorry to disturb you so late, but I have a problem.'

'Oh dear. Can I help?'

'You see, my boiler has broken and I wondered if could come and use your bath?'

What do you say when a single woman of a certain age asks a question like that?

WHAT DO YOU SAY!?

'Er . . .' was what I said.

We stood on the front step, with me metaphorically jiggling from foot to foot like a six-year-old standing waiting while his mum engages in one of those boring conversations with another mum on the way to the shops.

I was all but speechless.

'I know it's late. I'm sorry. But . . .'

'No, no. It's fine. Fine.'

'Honestly, it was silly of me to ask.'

Pause.

'But I've got no hot water. The plumber should be round tomorrow . . .'

'Sure,' I said. Sure? I was sure it was a lie. It had to be a lie. She didn't want just a bath. She wanted a bath and . . . well, I shan't go there.

'And I need to wash my hair for tomorrow's classes.' Pause. 'I know it's late. Sorry.' But she wasn't budging.

'OK. But you'll need to be quick, as I am about to turn in for the night. But OK.'

'I'll be back in five minutes.'

'OK.'

Had I just invited her in for sex? Or rather, did she think I had just invited her in for sex? Because I certainly hadn't.

What she didn't know was that I had guests. I was with Rachel and her husband Chris, two neighbours who had dropped by with some pictures the girls had painted round at their house earlier in the day.

I shut the door and went back into the sitting room. Rachel had her hand over her mouth to stop herself from shrieking with giggles. 'Jeremy, what was that all about? What was THAT all about!? She comes round here asking for a bath!? Is she out of her mind!?'

'Er. Probably. Yes. She may well have been asking for a bath, but I can't help feeling she wanted something else!'

'And?'

'Well, I said she could come round. For a bath.'

'But not "something else"?'

'What do you mean?'

'For sex?'

'No way!'

'This is so strange! Are you having an affair with her?'

'NO WAY!'

'There's you, a single man, and her, a single woman. Whyever not?' And she and her husband burst out laughing. Well, actually, she was rolling around on the sofa.

There was a knock at the door.

There, in a bathrobe, at ten o'clock on a Sunday evening, was a single woman of a certain age who I barely knew Coming to My House for a Bath. I assume she had nothing on underneath her robe. I assume she didn't just want a bath.

I introduced her to Rachel and Chris, who she didn't know even though they lived round the corner. I wasn't quite sure how I should handle this, but I am sure I handled it better because they were there. I took her up to the bathroom, turned on the taps, etc., and padded downstairs.

I wonder what she was thinking while she took her bath?

No, I can't. I daren't go there.

Sam came downstairs shortly afterwards, washed and scrubbed, her hair all frizzed after she'd towelled it dry. The four of us chatted for about one minute and then she went off into the night, with Rachel and Chris, chuckling, leaving shortly after.

I knew it would be all round the street by the time the school bell rang tomorrow. That was the problem: I was living under a microscope, my every move watched – most solicitously – by half the neighbourhood.

I had to get out.

20

'That man behaves as if he has a red-hot chilli pepper up his bum,' a friend once quipped in reference to me. I have never been a restful person, but after Lizzie's death it was as if I was on some adrenaline kick. I pushed myself very hard and I was always anticipating some crash landing, which so far hasn't happened.

Four months later, after I had returned to work full-time, I switched jobs within my department, so I had a completely new brief to master. Within a few weeks of that, I was seconded onto some BBC think tank, which, for its three-month duration, was virtually a full-time job on top of the day job. Once we'd produced our report, doing just the day job, new brief and all, seemed a bit humdrum. In other words, I needed a change and I began to sniff around for something new. Then, in the spring of 1994, my dream job came up, running 10x10, a BBC 2 series of short films for new directors produced out of Bristol.

My room for manoeuvre in the job market was constrained by my circumstances, so the 10x10 gig in Bristol, less than a dozen miles from Maka and Deda in Bath, looked like it had been heaven sent.

Miraculously, I got it, even though my interview was somewhat compromised. I discovered the evening before that the children had taped *Fireman Sam* over half of the video showreel they had asked me to watch for the interview. So I blagged about films I hadn't seen. Nothing changes.

The sixth phase of grief is called the upward turn. This was my new start.

I told the children over breakfast.

'Girls, Daddy's got a new job.'

'That's nice, Daddy. What is it?'

'It's based in Bristol, so we will need to move to Bath, near to Maka and Deda.'

'That's nice. You do that, Daddy, and Luce and I will stay here,' said Jessica matter-of-factly, munching her Rice Krispies.

'I agree,' chimed in Lucy.

Good start, I thought.

I handed in my notice and put the Oxford house on the market, and every weekend we went to Bath looking for a new home.

Eventually, we found a nice one, just about afford-able, in the area we wanted, just down the hill from what was supposed to be the best primary school in town. The owners accepted my offer, but as they were in no hurry to move and I didn't have the money to move, we put everything on hold.

Then came two big snags: the best primary school in

town seemed to not want Jessica and Lucy to darken their doors and I couldn't sell the Oxford house.

Meanwhile, I started the new job, which meant driving from Oxford to Bristol and back nearly every day, which made my former daily commute to London feel like a piece of piss. One morning I was taking Jessica, Lucy and Joe Unia to school before the marathon journey and, as I turned right out of our street onto the main route into the city centre, snarled with rush-hour traffic, I collided with a motorcyclist. It was as much his fault as mine, but it was unnerving. 'Do you think your dad will go to prison?' said Joe. Well, of course not, but it made Jessica really anxious and I decided this couldn't go on, so I found the girls a school almost on the last day of the summer term, even though it wasn't terribly close to the new house, and I decided to take out a humungous loan so we could move to Bath full-time, regardless of whether or not we sold the Oxford house. I had mortgages worth over five times my salary, but who's counting? It's only money.

Even so, things didn't happen fast.

When school broke up we decamped to Bath for the summer holidays and returned to Oxford every weekend. Once term began we lived with Maka and Deda until we could move into the Bath house at half-term. And having said the fondest of farewells to Annette, I found another nanny – a loud, slightly scary, half-Chilean divorcee who looked like fun and had brought up two children of her own, so she obviously knew what she was doing. Or so

I reasoned. Unfortunately, Adriana didn't drive and the girls' new school was a couple of miles and/or a couple of bus rides from Maka and Deda, which was tough on everybody. Maka and Deda both seemed to treat her like a servant and, by keeping a very watchful eye on her, gave her no space. And even I had to upbraid her because she had allowed Jessica – now eight years old – to cook pancakes unsupervised. She apologized and I gave her one more chance. But it was rocky, even though she seemed to get on with Jessica and Lucy.

Then, a couple of weeks later, I got a call from Maka while I was at work. Adriana had poured water all over Lucy and had made her cry, and now she was under the kitchen table refusing to come out and hugging Lucy, who was not at all happy. Well, traumatized actually.

I asked to speak to Adriana. Eventually, after much off-line squawking, she came to the phone.

'What's going on?'

'You don't understand, Mr Howe.'

'What is there not to understand, Adriana? From what I hear, you have poured water all over Lucy and now you are terrorizing her under the kitchen table.'

'None of you understand.'

'Look, I am coming home right now. If you don't have a good explanation by the time I get back to Bath, you don't have a job. I'm sorry.'

By the time I got back, Adriana had left. The children were chattering away. 'Daddy, she poured water all over Lucy!'

'We were playing with our buckets in the bathroom and she just poured a whole bucket of cold water over me, Daddy.'

'Maka had to dry off her school sweatshirt on the Aga, Daddy.'

'Were you very upset, sweetie?'

'I was a bit. I didn't like it when she took me under the table.'

'Maka said it was Adriana's pills, Daddy.'

The next day, before work, I went round to her flat and paid her for the rest of the week.

'One day you will learn, Mr Howe. You have a lot to learn.' And she handed me a book. 'For you.' It was called *Learning to Forgive*. I just didn't need it, nor her piling guilt on me. The book sat accusingly – and unread – on my bedside table for a couple of weeks, then I threw it away.

So much for Nanny Number Three.

On to Nanny Number Four.

When Kerry came for her second interview, we were just moving into the new house in Bath.

I think of that move as a bit like *The Little House on the Prairie*, with me playing both Ma and Pa. We piled all our worldly belongings into a van, shut up the old, familiar, unsold house in Oxford and, on a whim of Pa's, set off into unknown territory on an adventure. It was a bit like my mother's move to Bromley when we left our father behind. Only, for me, it didn't feel like one long holiday this time, more like one bloody big gamble. New job (where no one knew me), new life (where no one knew me) and new mortgage (they certainly knew me). I've said that bringing up Jessica and Lucy has been my greatest achievement in life and, looking back, moving us to Bath was certainly a turning point in our return to normality. But as I doggedly unpacked all our stuff, it just felt like I had bitten off rather more than I could chew.

Kerry and I chatted and then she went upstairs to find the children. She later confided to one of my friends that she had found Jessica and Lucy rather aimlessly moving a pile of soft toys from one bed to the other, not really knowing how to organize their way out of chaos. 'I could be of some use here,' she thought, and she took the job.

Milly Molly Mandy, however, had one final test for Kerry. She had been shut in the house because she was new to it and we hadn't yet put butter on her paws. On the Sunday evening before Kerry started, I was putting out the rubbish and the cat darted between my legs into the back garden and stood there in the dark looking at me, swishing her tail triumphantly. I tried to cajole her back in with food, but instead she ran off. I stood for an age, calling out 'Milly Molly Mandy' like a pill, but she had vanished into the night. Bloody cat.

Next morning, it was the normal rush to get the girls off to school and me off to London for some meeting or other, but there was still no sign of the cat, only a plaintive mewing coming from somewhere outside. I dispatched the children off to the bottom of the garden (only thirty-three steps down to our lawn; more up, I reckoned) to hunt for her, but no luck, and we had to be off. We were walking (well, actually we never walked – we always raced, because I was always late) along the street to the car when Lucy spotted her.

'Look! Milly Molly Mandy!' And there she was, stuck up the palm tree at the end of our terrace and looking deeply miserable. She had got up but couldn't get down.

'Bloody cat,' I muttered. We stood at the bottom of the tree calling her, but all she did was mew.

'Oh dear. Um. Look, I tell you what – I'll have to take you to school and see if I can get her down before I go to work.'

'But, Daddy . . .'

'There's nothing we can do. Come on, darlings.'

I left the distressed cat and took two weeping girls to school. When I got back I rang the fire brigade – 'Sorry, mate, that's an RSPCA job' – then the RSPCA.

'How long has she been up there?'

'All last night.'

'Sorry, sir, we don't come out on cat rescues until they've been stuck up there forty-eight hours.'

'Oh.'

So I left a hastily scrawled note for Kerry, whose first day this was. 'Welcome, Kerry! Slight problem. Cat up tree. Can you fix please. J.' And went off to London.

When I got back at about 7 p.m. I was greeted by said bloody cat, two children hopping with glee and Kerry.

'Daddy, Kerry was ever so clever. She rescued Milly Molly Mandy!'

'How on earth?'

'I hailed a passing BT van with a ladder on its roof and offered him ten quid to get her down. She didn't half struggle though,' she said, matter-of-factly. We had found our Mary Poppins, and all for ten quid extra. Kerry had passed the Milly Molly Mandy retrieval test with full marks. She was unflappable.

I always made it a point of principle that the girls would visit me at work once every half-term and once in the school holidays. Firstly, because they enjoyed it (what child wouldn't? I worked as part of the unit that made the Wallace and Gromit films and we had a viewing room lined floor to ceiling with cartoons and short films. 'Is your job really to watch all these films, Daddy?' 'Kind of.' 'Coooool.') and secondly, to make sure my boss knew what I was up against.

I would take them and Kerry would come over to my office to pick them up.

My south London streetwise graduate secretary, with a dyed white forelock like Cruella de Vil, said of Kerry, as she left with the children running behind her, 'Blimey, I wouldn't get on the wrong side of her.' Six foot tall, leather bomber jacket, long dark-brown hair, built like a street-fighter's gal and very direct. Whenever she said, 'Come on, girls. Time to go,' the children would obey. Instantly. You didn't mess with Kerry. But the children doted on her, Maka and Deda called her 'our angel' and she was such a brilliant nanny that she survived with us until after the birth of her first child, and it was only when she was pregnant with her second and Jessica was about to sit her GCSEs that we parted company. She was, as she said, 'of some use'.

The great advantage of my new job was that I could take the girls to school nearly every day, pick them up from school regularly and eat supper with them once or twice a week. I would feel lonely waiting at the school gate with the other mums, all of whom knew each other – just as I had come to know the Oxford mums – but who were all strangers to me here. There was one man who regularly picked up a girl from Lucy's class. I found it a bit odd. A man at the school gate! Was he a perv, or a gay dad, or what (well, he had a pierced ear, what can you expect)? I realized that even though I didn't know them, I was beginning to see myself as a mother, like all the other mothers, and it never occurred to me that, just like him, I must have stood out like a sore thumb.

I had travelled a long way in two years.

Jessica would never do sleepovers. Lucy was as happy as a cricket to go and sleep with friends. Jessica absolutely would not.

She would happily sleep at Maka and Deda's, with or without me, she was happy to sleep anywhere at all, as long as it was with me, she would even tolerate babysitters, as long as it was a) Maka, b) one of the Unias or c) Linda, Annette or Kerry. No one else need apply.

Her younger sister would go off with her sleeping bag rolled tightly in a carrier bag without a murmur, but Jessica would stay put, with a rather stoic, stony stare and an uncharacteristic silence. She then turned it round to being time with Daddy alone, not that Lucy cared. Her no sleepover rule was as immutable as one of the Ten Commandments: the sky is blue, day follows night and Jessica doesn't do sleepovers.

Oh, and nobody knew or was to know. Because she was embarrassed about it.

'Does Lucy want to come over for a sleepover with Esther on Saturday night?'

'Yes, I'm sure she'd love to.'

'Jessica can come too.'

'Er. Sorry. No can do. She has homework to do. It's the Sabbath and she's not allowed out. She's climbing Everest and I'm not expecting her back till late.' I had run out of plausible excuses.

Once, when we were still in Oxford, I tried to get her to go. It was not a success.

A birthday party was on the horizon, a birthday party which involved An Adventure – i.e. a walk along the Berkshire Downs with an overnight in a youth hostel. In March. Sounded more like a penance to me, but I guess they all saw it as An Adventure. And Jessica – who was Becca's special friend (even though, for Jessica, Becca was emphatically not her special friend, she was just someone she happened to go to school with; oh dear) – was most definitely invited. I broached this with her, dressing it up as enormous fun, but of course she WOULD NOT GO. With six weeks' notice of this trek up the Amazon with no certainty of return, I gently told Becca's mum that we would be going away that weekend. 'Not to worry,' said Becca's mum. 'We'll change the date to suit you.' The whole thing seemed to revolve around Jessica. I tried suggesting a less ambitious project (just a walk, no sleepover), but no, Becca wanted An Adventure. I even resorted to telling the truth to her mum, but not even that cut any ice. 'I'm sure she'll be fine. We'll look after her. All children get a bit nervous about going away, don't they?' etc., etc.

But I stuck to the script and said no. So it was all off.

But then Jessica changed her mind. I don't recall her changing her mind ever, either before or since. She always was a child of immense certainty and whenever she showed signs of indecision, it was always a cue for trouble. And now she told Becca she would come along.

I offered to come along with her (a sacrifice of unparalleled generosity, both on my part and on Lucy's, who would then have had to tag along too). But no – she was going alone.

The week before the trek was a tad tense, but although she wavered a little every night, Jessica seemed determined to go ahead with it.

On the day – grey and wet – I walked round to Becca's

with her as if she were being led to an Olympic final. Tense, silent, like a hero from a Greek tragedy. Jessica and the Argonauts, Jessica auf Naxos – that kind of thing.

Lucy and I had a quiet day that Saturday. I was a) tense and b) expecting a phone call to rush down to Berkshire to pick up a traumatized child.

Julia came round. 'Any news?'

'None yet.'

Back to the fish fingers and an endless round of Frustration, which Lucy loved playing.

Sunday was the same.

'Any news?'

'Nothing.'

The house was like ground control in the film of *The Dam Busters* – the only sound was the clock ticking.

And then, mid-afternoon, she returned, wet and tired.

Triumphant?

No.

Grumpy.

Yes.

'I don't ever want to do that again. Ever.'

I have no idea what the trip had been like – 'I don't want to talk about it.' Nor did anyone else. Becca and her mother and the fellow sufferers all seemed to have signed a pact of silence.

Jessica never did a sleepover again. Which was both a brake on my social life (well, more like a full stop) and a looming problem for Jessica. I had visions of me as an old man shackled to Jessica, going to live with her at university because she didn't do sleepovers.

But then, just after she turned ten, we were forced to confront this particular elephant in the room.

In her final year at primary school in Bath, the big treat was a week-long stay at an activity centre on the Isle of Wight. Exactly the kind of thing my physically fearless older daughter would relish if only she could overcome her inner demons. I also thought that if she didn't go, it would magnify the problem of being away.

Besides, sitting alone in a classroom while the rest of her mates learnt to abseil and canoe would be so humiliating for her.

Not many people would say that being organized is my strongest suit, but in the summer holiday, ten months before the dreaded trip, I got in touch with Dr Forrest and explained my plight. Could she, would she, be able to help? She couldn't see us because we had moved out of her area, but she quickly referred me to a child psychiatrist in Bath who she was sure would do the trick.

So, once every three weeks, from the beginning of the autumn term in September, we would visit this poor man after school. Jessica would only go if Lucy went (please refer to page 170).

A typical session would go like this:

I sat opposite the doctor, say about three or four feet away, in his lovely, spacious, sun-lit office. Just in my eye-line, Lucy would be standing with her back to me, drawing endlessly on a large blackboard. Huddled in a corner was her sister, pretending to be deeply absorbed in her book.

The doctor and I would talk. Occasionally he would throw a direct question to Jessica, something innocuous, like, 'What do you enjoy most about school, Jessica?'

Long pause punctuated only by the scratch of Lucy's chalk on the board. Somebody mumbled something.

Lucy then said something like, 'Jessica says she enjoys reading and writing most of all,' while continuing with her drawing.

'Lucy, why do you think Jessica won't talk to the doctor?' I asked.

She stopped drawing, said, 'That's not fair of you. You know why,' and went back to her drawing.

This went on for seven torturous months.

And do you know what? Jessica did go to her adventure camp. And she never resorted to the doggedly achieved dispensation I wrung out of the school – she never used the phone there to tell me that she was homesick.

Saying farewell to her as she boarded the school bus was painful and the week she was away was an eternity.

At mealtimes Lucy and I sat in silence. 'I think it is Jessica who does all the talking, don't you, Daddy?'

The bus home arrived bang on time and there was Jessica, descending the steps and calmly walking towards me, expressionless. At the very last moment she flung her arms round me and hugged me. 'I did it, Daddy,' she whispered. I felt so proud of her.

Three years later she went on a school trip to China. When her best friend dropped out – 'Because she has a peanut allergy, Daddy, and they cook with peanuts in China' – she still went.

She went off to uni, not happily, I have to admit, but she went, and I didn't have to live with her there. Miracle-workers come in many guises: that poor doctor must have done something!

21

Eighteen months after we moved to Bath I made a film about Lizzie's death. It was like walking up to Medusa and looking at her full in the face.

It didn't break me. But it did change me.

Out of the blue, the series I was running for BBC Bristol was decommissioned. I was summoned to see my boss (much like my old boss but tougher, gruffer, more streetwise, more telly – 'The kind of boss who can fillet out your backbone and you'd thank him for it,' said one of his former staff). Instead of curtains ('Thank you for all your hard work but I am going to have to lose you, Jeremy,' which is what I was expecting/dreading), he said, 'I want you to work alongside Peter Symes and co-produce *Picture This*. He is going away for two or three months and I need someone to keep his seat warm. Are you interested?' *Picture This* was the most prestigious series BBC Bristol was then making for BBC2, a run of authored thirty-minute documentaries.

You bet, I thought. 'Yes. Sounds good to me,' I said.

'Oh, and you'd have to direct a film for the series.'

Shit, shit and double shit. Was this Christmas, was I hallucinating, or what?

'OK. Fine.'

'Have you directed for telly before?'

'Er . . . No. I've mainly produced.'

'Here's your chance.'

Pause.

'How do you feel?'

'Excited. Nervous . . .'

'It'll be nerve-wracking, but you'll learn a lot. Good luck.'

Not quite the meeting I was expecting.

I spent the weekend coming up with ideas and on Monday afternoon I met Peter in his cubbyhole of an office in an attic at BBC Bristol for 'a chat'. I had spoken with him a few times, but I hardly knew him. His reputation was pretty extraordinary: 'legend' kind of sums it up. Peter Symes, the patron saint of serious documentary television. We chatted about this and that, and then he asked me what film I would like to make for his series. I pitched various ideas, but I could sense his complete lack of interest.

'Any other ideas floating around, my dear chap?'

I paused.

'Do you know Shakespeare's *The Winter's Tale*?'

'Yes?' he said, in a way that means, 'No, not really. Remind me.'

I pitched the story of the play that had found a way into my heart, telling him of the last production I had seen with Lizzie and how I thought the transformation scene with the statue, which is, for me, one of Shakespeare's greatest achievements, just hadn't worked.

'Yes?' he questioned, in the kind of tone that suggested that he thought this drama luvvie had lost the plot of documentary television. 'And why do you want to make this?'

'In my last job I was offered a production of the play. It is the play I most wanted to direct, but I just didn't know how to make that statue move, so I bottled out of it. I do now.'

'Yes, but why?'

And then I told him my story, the story of this book, and his earnest, piercing blue eyes lit up, he leaned forward, and, like the doctor in that surgery in Norfolk nearly four years before, I could see that his jaw was about to drop.

'I want to bring Lizzie back to life.'

'But how?'

And then I told him about *La Jetée*.

Late one night, at a film festival in France the year before, slightly drunk and overtired, I saw *La Jetée*, a cult French short made in the sixties, which was later used as the basis for *Twelve Monkeys*. My French is only good enough for me to have got the gist rather than fully comprehend it. It tells of how a man who survives a nuclear holocaust is trained by fellow survivors to travel into the future to get help, but to learn to travel into the future he needs first to learn to travel into the past. It is a clever conceit and is, of course, a film about memory, the memory of a love affair he once had. Uniquely for a movie, it is all shot in black and white stills. Two thirds of the way through this twenty-eight-minute film, the hero remembers one afternoon when he and his girlfriend made love and there are shots of her lying on her side, her head propped up by her elbow. She is looking straight at the camera. And then she blinks. *She blinks*. In a film made entirely from still photographs, she comes to life and blinks. This, the one and only moving image, is about a second long. As I sat in the cinema, it blew my mind. That one device had brought the past back to life, had brought the past into the present. Just as I wanted to make Lizzie a part of my present. If only I could find a way to bring Lizzie back. The film left me in a daze. It haunted me. It was like a dream. And now I wanted to remake it about Lizzie.

I wanted to bring Lizzie to life, if only for a second.

'I see,' he said. 'That's clever.'

I got the gig.

It became an obsession. But film-making is an obsession – making a good film is so hard that unless you are obsessed it is just not worth doing.

For four months I was in the grip of it, my mission to bring Lizzie back to me.

I scoured the south of England for the remotest, most desolate locations, cast doubles to play me and Jessica and Lucy and we filmed figures trekking across winter landscapes or standing alone in endless muddy fields.

I hired a car and a double which had been wrecked in an accident and we filmed the image I had been carrying in my head since Lizzie died – of a smashed-up car with all of our belongings – papers, books, photos, fluffy toys, luggage –

strewn across a fog-bound landscape. The three of us were looking on, bewildered.

We filmed Wittenham Clumps, we filmed mist-shrouded, uprooted trees, ice-covered puddles, sleet falling against grey skies: we filmed bleakness whenever we could find it.

We filmed the dripping of a tap, rain coursing down windows, the actors playing the three of us waving off the train from Oxford Station, Jessica's double saying her prayers.

Nearly every exterior was shot in rain or in fog. And in nearly every shot there were photographs of Lizzie: scattered in fields, on car seats, against train windows, reflected in windscreens.

We filmed Lizzie's beloved books and papers laid out on her desk in soft, warm light – the books and diaries in which I just couldn't find her, could not get her back.

I went to Oxford to interview Catherine Unia, Dr Hall and my sister Philippa. All of them were very tense about the ordeal they'd signed up for.

I asked Philippa how she remembered Lizzie and me.

'I remember one Christmas when we were all opening our presents at our mother's house and you had given Lizzie a clock or something and as she opened it I remember the look between you across the crowded room. That look just summed it up. Nobody else existed. Just you two, Lizzie and Jeremy. You were a pair, you were strong and when you two were together everyone felt a bit locked out because you really were together . . . '

I felt my chest tighten. I don't know if I remembered the moment or if, in that instant that my sister spoke, I reconstructed it, but I could see Lizzie opening my present, the Heal's clock with its simple face and its wooden case which stood on our mantelpiece still, even though it had given up the ghost years ago, and I could see and feel across that noisy room, full of our family feverishly absorbed in the unwrapping of their presents, the smile in her eyes that bonded us. Lizzie and Jeremy. That is who we were, who I was, who I should be. Together I always felt that Lizzie and I could conquer the world. One word defines what gave us that strength. Love. Inexplicable, irrational, incomprehensible, overwhelming: love. And there in that hushed hotel room I felt Lizzie and Jeremy were as far away from me as the most distant star in the night sky. Visible, but unreachable. A bright light emanating from a source that in all likelihood had ceased to exist. Real and unreal. We had lost so much. And at that moment the pain of that loss made me feel as if my heart was about to burst.

'. . . and in agreeing to be in the film,' Philippa continued, 'you've made me remember things I wanted to put away and to forget. I have had to open a drawer full of memories of the time that Lizzie was killed and to look at them again, and to be honest I can't wait to get home and repack them and close the drawer and lock it shut . . .'

I felt envious. As Philippa said it I realized that I had huge, ugly heaps of memories strewn everywhere, a mess of wreckage blocking my view of the past and my path into the future, fouling up the present, polluting everything. Stinking piles of festering garbage poisoning my water supply. I wanted to shout out, 'You lucky bastard! Look at me neck deep in this shit.' Instead –

'What do you remember about the day of Lizzie's funeral?' and the bile in my throat receded and the cameraman called 'Cut' because he needed to reload the camera and I rushed off to the toilet to try to calm myself.

I was interviewed for the film, too. To be honest I couldn't think how I could spin out my paltry handful of images to last more than about five minutes. I needed something to fill up the other twenty-four minutes and fifteen seconds between the opening and closing credits and I was the only person I could think of to tell the story.

I could hardly interview myself could I, so I asked another Philippa (not my sister, but a mate) to do it for me. She happens to be the best documentary interviewer I have ever come across, so when she said, 'Yes, of course, I'd be honoured,' I felt I might just have a film on my hands.

She interviewed me in the kitchen of our house in Bath. It was like being in a confessional, a gruelling three hours sitting there in the cold gloom of my house (the boiler was making so much noise the sound recordist had insisted we turn it off, even though it was January), reliving the misery of what happened to us in front of the six earnest people who were my crew. It was horribly public.

'If it hurts, it's real,' I said, 'the only way I have felt real since Lizzie died is if I hurt and I've hurt so much over the last three years.'

I was just about holding back my tears.

'Just because someone's dead doesn't mean you stop loving them. And that is hard. It's tough. I think something of me was murdered that day.'

I gripped my chair tighter and tighter. My knuckles went white. I was weeping now, but I didn't care.

'Essentially Lizzie and I were the same person, so losing her was like having my arm ripped out, and the damage that causes is massive, *massive*, the shock waves are immense, and I wonder just how much damage we have sustained: that day I lost more than I can bear, more than I can bear . . . and grief is a black hole that sucks everything into it and it can destroy everything. It's not a pleasant place to be in, but it's also a fascinating place to be in. It's unmissable in a way. Grief is unlike anything else. The whole world is different. You see the whole world through a different set of spectacles. You are on Planet Grief. I am sure I am a stronger person for what I have been through. I have seen people blown away by grief – you see other people suffering grief, and it touches a button, it opens a wound, and then I think thank God, I am not still in that awful place.'

After three hours of this, we broke for lunch, interrogation over, and walked to a pub round the corner.

'Jeremy,' Philippa asked, 'why on earth are you making this film?'

'I . . . Er . . . Well, I thought it would be cathartic.'

'Jeremy, catharsis happens in Greek tragedy, not in lives like yours or mine. You chump.'

I was chastened, but it was way too late to turn back. I was roped up and climbing a treacherous rock face with my team. I had to get to the summit.

You might recall that John Hall had suggested in our sessions that I needed to put going back to York on the agenda. So, hiding behind the guise of making the film, I decided to go to the room where Lizzie had been killed. It would be the climax of the film.

When I interviewed him, I mentioned this to John. 'Hm. When I said to go back to York, I didn't quite anticipate you going there with a film crew and visiting the room where Lizzie died.' I think his subtext was, 'Have you lost your mind, mate?'

'I see.'

'It's a bit extreme.'

It was a bit extreme for the University of York too. They flatly refused me permission to film. I resorted to coercion, not far short of blackmail. Peter Symes was a friend of the Vice Chancellor's wife, and he leant on her. I, meanwhile, wrote a stinker of a letter to the press office – and copied in everybody who was anybody at the university – stating that if they refused me permission I would both include that refusal in the finished film and use footage from the local BBC TV archive to drag the university through the mud.

Not a nice tactic, but it worked. They phoned my researcher and gave us permission to film in the room, but on the condition that I did not reveal the exact identity and location of the room, and only if I could complete all the filming by the end of the week. It was a Tuesday. We booked ourselves in at eleven on Friday morning. I had three days to prepare.

We hastily assembled the crew and on Thursday after lunch we set out for York to film the next day. It was a grim journey; we were a bit like Frodo and co approaching Mount Doom. As we approached York, I got more and more morose. John Hall had been right – what in God's name was I doing this for?

The next day, we spent the morning filming at York Station, where Lizzie had arrived for the summer school, with me in a black taxi imagining Lizzie's last journey up to the campus. Time dragged by and then, at about a quarter to eleven, we asked the taxi driver to take us to the university, where we were met by a hapless press officer outside the block where Lizzie died. It was the vacation and the place was utterly deserted.

And it was sleeting.

This was always going to be a one-hit wonder – you can film a man going to the scene of his wife's death for the first time only once. There can be no retakes. My researcher and the cameraman went up to the room with the press officer to check it out, while I sat in the taxi trying to blank out what I was about to do. Recce done and room unlocked, they reported back, and suddenly I was on the runway ready for take-off. It was as if I were acting, that I was only pretending this was happening to me. I knew I needed to look sombre, so I thought sombre, and while I was thinking sombre, we were off. I wasn't really thinking about what I was going through. I was protecting myself by thinking about how I looked on film. I deliberately trudged up the stairs because it helped my cameraman and sound recordist, who were walking up the stairs backwards filming me – and, also, don't sombre people trudge?

We reached the top of the stairs, walked along the corridor and I waited by the door as if I were expecting a signal. Then I pushed it open and walked into the room where Lizzie had been murdered.

What had I been expecting?

It was just a plain, freshly painted, empty university study bedroom on the top floor of a 1970s student block, and although I knew the university well, it was not at all how I had imagined it.

At first it was just a room, but as I stood there and thought about what I was doing, it became the bleakest, loneliest place in the universe, even with three of us and a camera crowded into a small space.

Lizzie was not there.

As I stood looking round the room, I tried to enact in my head the events of her death, but my mind couldn't – wouldn't – go there. I could imagine her sitting at her desk working, I could imagine the knock on the door and

I could imagine not Lizzie, but only Lizzie about to be killed. Then my mind just stopped.

And I started to weep.

It was the last place on earth where Lizzie was and I wanted her to be there so badly. But she was not there and all I could feel was a fog of sadness and loneliness. I physically hurt. I wanted to leave, but instead I sat at her desk and buried my face in my hands and wept, dimly aware of the two people unsure of quite how to cope with the wretched scene they were trying to film. I wanted to be with Lizzie, but Lizzie just wasn't there. I wanted to jump off this cliff, this summit of awfulness, and sink into oblivion.

Instead I stood up, wiped the snot and the tears away and said, 'Let's go.' I took one last look at this meaningless, existential space and before I knew it I was outside being hugged by my PA and my researcher.

'It was awful.'

'You look wiped out.'

'I feel terrible. I feel like I have just come out of battle.'

I was speechless. I was in shock.

I sat in the taxi while they sorted out things with the press officer and the cameraman did some pick-up shots, and then we drove home. I slept the whole length of the journey back.

I didn't find Lizzie there, but I could at least imagine her death in a way that I had never been quite able to do before then, and I think I wished I couldn't. In that small room I encountered the deepest misery I have ever had to confront and a loneliness, both mine and mine for Lizzie, that was just utter darkness. The wastefulness of what happened there, the tragedy for Lizzie. I got closer to her death. Her murder. The evil done to her. I'd thought that if I could confront her death, I could bring back her life. That didn't happen, but I had survived an ordeal.

I have never returned to York since.

Then I had to edit the damn thing. I had four weeks, which was generous. Week one was fun: we assembled bits of it and gave it a loose structure. Then I went away, which pleased the editor – 'I can get the scissors into the final section when you visit The Room.'

When I came back, he had reduced the room sequence from twelve minutes (which is how long my awful visit had taken) to about ten. Watching seals being clubbed to death would have been more edifying than this ten minutes of unalloyed misery. We sliced our way into it, cutting it down to about two horribly raw minutes of programme.

Week two was difficult, but it was lightened by the fact that it was half-term and every day the girls came with me to the edit suite. While Pete (the film editor) and I cut our film, they busied themselves with making their own films, which they loved.

Week three was tougher – the girls were back at school and we had narrowed down our options – but week four was unbelievably hard, because we needed to show this private weep-fest to my various bosses, which left me feeling raw as hell, and also because we had to precisely define every image, every beat, to tell the story. Film is unforgiving in its logic: a good film flows unimpeded like water, it has a rhythm to it. It is not like writing prose or making conversation, which can digress, even go round in circles, and still work. It is a medium for clear, crisp, uncluttered thinking.

Editing the film to a fine cut forced me to make order out of the chaos caused by Lizzie's death. It took me as close to breaking point as I had ever been before, but at eight o'clock on Friday of week four, the film was completed.

A couple of evenings later, at our house, I showed the finished film to Maka. It is full of still images of Lizzie and it keeps returning to one slightly mystifying photograph in which she is looking away from the camera. At the point where I am left marooned in The Room, the film cuts to a half-screen shot of that image, which morphs until it fills the whole screen. At that point, Lizzie turns and looks directly into the camera, and then the picture freezes again and fades to silver raindrops on a window. It is a video grab from the only footage I have of Lizzie and I had designed the whole film – called *A Moving Image* – around that closing four-second clip at the end of the film. The statue comes to life.

As she watched the closing moments, Maka just murmured, 'Oh my Lizzie' and hugged me.

There in our cosy sitting room, which overlooks Bath – the city she called home – spread out below us, surrounded by my and Lizzie's books, with our children safely asleep in their beds upstairs, our cat dozing on the sofa, Lizzie turns round and looks at us. Through the artifice of film, at the moment when I force us to confront the awful reality of her murder, she is here with us. Her fine, dark-chestnut hair, her warm, loving brown eyes, a smile of love and affection, Lucy sitting smugly on her lap looking content and happy – Lizzie, my darling, darling Lizzie, was there with us. I felt her warmth, her love, her contentedness. I felt our marriage, our bond in life. I saw her beauty, I could smell her soft, flawless skin, I recall her stammering, rapid speech, her fierce, restless intelligence, her directness. The simplicity, the Lizzieness of her is with me. I am so happy that I cry and Maka just repeats and repeats, 'My darling, darling girl,' and then the moment is gone, but I shall have it in my heart for ever.

I had stared at the gorgon and I had triumphed.

Exhausted, I took the best part of a month off work and pottered. I built some shelves, did some gardening (me, gardening! Bloody hell!) and recharged my batteries. I felt like I was recovering from shellshock.

It gave me the chance to reflect on what had happened to us. Were we damaged by Lizzie's death? I looked at my cousin, whose father had died, whose mother had appeared to be coping but who'd fallen apart – she had plenty of money, rarely worked and drank her way out of sorrow. Was her mother damaged by her husband's death? I think she was.

I looked at a former colleague. He had been having an affair, was driving home from Birmingham to his family in Stratford late one night along a dual carriageway when a man ran out in front of him. He hit him and killed him instantly. My colleague's life fell to pieces. I remember him sitting in my office:

'I look at you and you are still standing. What happened to you was far worse, but I'm a wreck and you are not. Why?'

Is it the luck of the gods, the luck of the draw? Yes and no. I had two children to bring up. I had a reason to get up every morning and I had to earn a living – there was no other way to support our lives. Pick yourself up, dust yourself down and move forward. You have to do what you have to do. But while his life was perhaps built on sand, I had secure foundations. That said, I still don't really know the answer to his desperate question.

And the girls? A few months after Lizzie's death, Karin and David came round to lunch and Jessica and Lucy had two friends, sisters the same age as my two, round to play. As I made the lunch (notice I don't use the word 'cook'), Karin was watching the four of them out in the garden. Jessica was busy telling everyone what to do and Lucy was being her able lieutenant.

'Do you know, Jeremy, if I didn't know otherwise, if asked to choose, I would say that it was not your two who had been through a tragedy, but the girls they are playing with. Jessica and Lucy are very sure of themselves and their place in the world.'

Karin was right. But when I look at the girls now and see the normal, well-adjusted young women they have become, I touch wood and cross my fingers, for it might have been so different.

And Lizzie? I have dreamt of Lizzie only three times since she died, but those dreams have stayed with me for months, as if she had just walked back into my life. Just as all her books are mixed in with my books on the shelves that line most of the rooms in our house, so her life is mixed in with ours. I am currently reading *Madame Bovary*; it is the copy Lizzie bought during our finals (most of the rest of us would have idly flicked through *The Sun* or *OK* magazine as distraction from exams. Not Lizzie, who elected to read one of the key nineteenth-century texts – because it is French and not English, somehow she didn't see it as work). We still use the blue and white kitten mug the girls gave her for her last birthday. She is an invisible part of our lives. I see her in the way that Lucy wipes her nose and when she sits down to play the cello, when she concentrates, I could be looking at Lizzie. I have a photograph by my desk of Lizzie aged seven – every time I look at it I do a double-take because I think it is Jessica. Not only are they identical (although Jessica doesn't really resemble her mother at all now), but the way Lizzie is looking into the middle-distance, deep in thought, is identical to the way Jessica used to stand at that age. And it is weird when Jessica behaves in a way that is emotionally identical to her mother: when she was studying for her GCSEs, it was like having Lizzie in the house. No one can tell me there is no such a thing as a revising gene.

I think of Lizzie every day. Every single day since she died I have thought of her, and sometimes I have a ridiculous worry that if she came back she wouldn't know where to find us because we have moved, that she wouldn't recognize Jessica and Lucy because they have changed. And if Lizzie were still alive what would we all be doing now? It would have been very different, I am sure, but I am convinced that it would be neither worse nor better.

But although Lizzie lives on in my heart and in our memories, she will never come back, and our lives together, or rather our life together, feels as if it happened to another person, not me, but another, very different Jeremy Howe. I am not damaged, but I am changed. Lizzie wasn't just damaged, she was destroyed.

A few months after we made the final cut, the film was broadcast. I made sure I was out of the country on our summer holiday. It had a mixed reaction. Deda hated it. The relationship I was in, already a bit iffy, hit a rock after the film (my girlfriend's father saw the film and said, 'He deserves to be horse-whipped'). Some of the reviewers thought it was dreadful, but most admired it for its searing honesty. I also got the largest postbag I have ever received for a programme, by about several hundred letters. One did call it self-indulgent and excremental, but the rest were blown away by it and thanked me for sharing my story.

I never showed my film to the girls. I had edited a copy

without any of the really graphic bits about the murder, in case they wanted to see it, but they never asked.

And my interviewer, Philippa, was wrong. It *was* cathartic. I was a changed person. The heaps of shit I had been wrestling with while I edited the film had indeed been put into some kind of order. I packed my baggage away and shut the drawer and, lighter, I moved on. I really did.

22

The seventh phase of grief is about acceptance and hope. My story has a happy ending. A very happy ending.

Once upon a time, I used to be a theatre director. When Lizzie was pregnant with Jessica and I was a freelancer earning next to nothing, she suggested that I needed a proper job. So I left the theatre and joined the BBC (actually, it wasn't that easy, but this is a happy story).

Fast forward ten years and my old boss from the theatre called me, out of the blue.

'Jeremy, I am looking for a Scottish woman to direct a show for me, so I thought of you,' and he laughed.

So a couple of months after *A Moving Image* was aired, I took unpaid leave from the BBC and off I went to Perth in Scotland to direct Terrence Rattigan's *In Praise of Love*, a beautiful play about a middle-aged couple faced with the wife's terminal illness, a play about trying to cope with loss before it happens. I wonder why I was the Scottish woman director he was looking for!

My three-week stay in Perth was the longest I had been apart from the girls.

My fortieth birthday fell while I was away, so Jessica

and Lucy, accompanied by Kerry, were coming up for my birthday weekend. I arranged for them to be off school for three days, gave them a small fortune for sweets and comics for their epic train journey and set them a quiz of things to look out for from the window. Early on Thursday evening, tired but excited, they arrived in Scotland for the first time in their lives.

On Friday they pottered while I rehearsed.

On Saturday morning they came with me to work and, while I rehearsed, they went with my stage manager and tried on all the costumes being made for the pantomime which was the theatre's next show. After lunch, with rehearsals over for the week, we drove to Edinburgh, stopping on the way at the aquarium (with sharks) by the Forth Bridge, walked down Princes Street and gawped at the shops, went for a ride on the carousel by the National Gallery and had a slap-up fortieth birthday supper at Pizza Hut on the Royal Mile. Tired but elated, we drove back to Perth – and Jessica, Lucy and Kerry went to bed. I stayed up and watched a film.

Sleepless in Seattle came out the year after Lizzie was killed. I avoided it. Friends would say, 'Jeremy, you have to see *Sleepless in Seattle*, it is so like you. Well, on second thoughts, maybe you shouldn't see it. In fact you definitely shouldn't see it.' So I hadn't. Until I finally watched it late that November evening, in a flat in Perth, where I was staying while I directed a play about love. It blew me away. As I wept over the closing credits, I rang Jennie.

Jennie?

Jennie and I had been introduced that spring by Karin and David over Sunday lunch at their cottage in Somerset. Jennie had been en route from the National Film and Television School in the home counties, where she taught, to her cottage in north Devon, where she lived, and she joined us. She had been a film producer – real films, movies that you pay money to see in cinemas, not poxy bits of TV like mine – had got fed up with the hassle of The Business and had retired to write and do a bit of teaching.

It was a lovely lunch. I have no reason to think that Karin and David were matchmaking, but Jennie and I got on rather well. We made a vague arrangement to meet later in the summer when we were, by coincidence, going on holiday with my sister and mother and co to north Devon for a week. It seemed silly not to see her while we were there. I phoned her from the holiday cottage we had rented, but she wasn't in. I sent her a card and thought no more about it, but the card she sent in return seemed as if she was inviting herself over: 'A friend of mine has a stack of girls' books she has no use for. Would your girls like them? Love Jennie x.'

We had lunch. She gave two boxes of books (and some posh chocolates) to the children, who squirrelled them away. 'Daddy, what shall we do now?'

'Why don't you play?'

'Just play?'

'Yes, just play,' and they scampered off upstairs and just played while Jennie and I chatted. We certainly did get on.

A couple of weeks later we had supper.

The following week we arranged for her to pick me up from London after a morning screening of a short film I was working on and drive me back to Bath, as she was staying with her brother, who lived in a village not far from us.

We met at the cutting room at 11 a.m. that Friday morning. What I didn't tell her until a year later was that my screening had been cancelled at about 10 p.m. the evening before – 'Film's in no state to be seen, Jeremy mate. Sorry' – so I had travelled down to London early simply to get a lift back home with Jennie. It was during the journey that it all happened between us and then almost instantly I was off to Perth.

'Were you watching *Sleepless in Seattle*?' I now asked her over the phone.

'Of course I was,' she sobbed. And for the next two hours we talked and talked.

And I fell in love on the day before my fortieth birthday. At the age of 39 and 364 days I knew what love is. This wasn't an affair, this was the real thing. Jennie was beautiful, clever as you come, witty, charming and, for all her exotic past – she'd been married to a jazz trumpeter, divorced him, changed her career in her thirties from teaching to producing, via writing and directing, had worked in Hollywood and had produced a string of classy movies, from comedy to art house – she was incredibly like me. We were both ordinary, sensible, middle-class English graduates, who had somehow found themselves in the mad world of films. I know this sounds facetious, but sitting in the garden with Karin, David and Jennie that Sunday afternoon, with the children trying to do handstands against the garden wall, when Jennie said how much she liked baking cakes – this person, who was one of the most successful women film producers in the country, liked baking cakes! – I kind of knew that Jennie was someone special. And she was such good fun, *is* such good fun. Basically, we had a lot to talk about because we had so much in common.

A few weeks later we moved in together. There wasn't the slightest doubt in my mind, not a moment of hesitation; even though we had known each other for no more than a couple of months it was the easiest decision of my life. I recall what my wise sound recordist on *A Moving Image* said to me about his wife of thirty years – he regretted that they hadn't married sooner. When you know you are in love just act on it – and Jennie and I did. For me, it was like coming home: our house became a home for the first time in four and a half years, my life became normal and we became a family, and all because of Jennie. Jeremy, Jessica, Lucy and Jennie: our family. I put my past in the drawer that Philippa had told me about, along with the wedding ring Lizzie had given me, and moved forward, no longer a widower but at last a normal person again. There will always be a part of my heart that is Lizzie's, but I was no longer locked into that past. What had seemed impossible just a few months before now seemed so natural and easy. Ordinary life beckoned. I just love ordinary life. The

Chinese proverb says, 'May you live in interesting times.'
I have absolutely no wish to live in interesting times.

And the happy ending? I am writing now by the ocean
in California, while Jennie, my darling wife of over ten
years, is asleep across the room. I found love and compan-
ionship and a proper family when I thought all those things
had been snatched from me for ever. Jennie has been a
brilliant mother to Jessica and Lucy, who are women now:
the reason I am in California is that Lucy is at university
in San Diego and Jessica has taken a week out from her job
as an assistant producer at a radio station to hang out with
us. My life is back on track, my career too, and I am happy
and contented in a way that I never thought would be possible after that dreadful day in July 1992. I hear the wind
in the rigging of yachts as I walk by the harbour down the
road and I am reminded of the storm that blasted our lives,
leaving me clinging onto to Jessica and Lucy for dear life
as I tried to steer my way through chaos. But it is just a
memory now, and I have been allowed to move forward.
I am not going to write about the present, my life now, my
wonderful marriage, my grown-up, beautiful daughters,
full of poise and grace. My story is of one long moment
from the past and how it helped forge us, Jessica, Lucy
and me. We were not damaged, just changed. To butcher
Wordsworth, it is a story of how the father was mother to
the women – my two beloved daughters.

Thanks

If Lizzie and I had a strategy – or a wish even – about bringing up the girls, and it is not something we ever spoke about apart from bickering about which secondary schools they should go to (me, the local comp; Lizzie, the local Girls' Day School Trust – in absentia, she won), I think it was that we wanted their childhood to be idyllic and for it to go on for as long as it possibly could. What happened to us in July 1992 hardly helped either come to pass, but I hope that the pages you have just read prove that, with a few compromises and a lot of improvisation, Jessica and Lucy and I didn't make a bad fist of it. Many people have remarked on how well I brought up my girls. Well, yes, I think I did, but with an enormous amount of love and care from friends, family, neighbours and experts. I think that if this book is about anything, it is about the strength of our family and the love and care and affection directed towards the Howes. I hope that it is a tribute to love and friendship in all its manifestations.

I want to thank everybody from the bottom of my heart, named and unnamed, most living but alas some dead, who reached out a helping hand to us in a time of need. Most particularly, to my mother, who is too ill to be able to read this, to my brother Jonathan and my sister Philippa, to Yvonne and Malcolm, Ethel and Mirko, Louise and David and to my cousin Liz. To the girls' godparents – chosen by Lizzie – Jane Weaver, her parents Inga-Stina and Roger Ewbank and her husband Sean, to Martin and Phyllis Hatfull, to Eoin O'Callaghan, Gill Manning, Rachel and Ian Kirk Smith and Sarah Mitchell and Robbie. To all our friends and neighbours – the Reads, the Unias, the Hooles, the Zawadas, the Brills and Bedells, the Goreings and Golds, the Byrnes, the Thoroughgoods, the Pauls, the Huxleys, the Gledhills, the Tamblings, the Walls, the Hurrels, the Kennedys and more – who just scooped us up in myriad ways. To the various manifestations of boss that thread the narrative – to David Rose and Karin Bamborough, to Michael Winter, John Tydeman, Colin Rose, Jeremy Gibson and Peter Symes – and to colleagues, especially the late Kate Poulton and her family, to Clive Brill, Alexa Moore, Henry Dagg, Janet Whitaker and Cherry Cookson, Rebecca Wilmshurst, Jeremy Mortimer, Elaine Bedell, Philippa Lowthorpe, Val Mitchell, Isabel Pritchard, Jonathan Collinson Bloom, John Wilson and Peter Brownlee. To our nannies, Annette and Kerry, to Drs Forrest, Hall, Ganz, Potter and Rathbone, to Jessica and Lucy's friends and their mums and to their teachers – Mr Townsend, Mr Standish, Mrs Nauman, Ms Draper, Elizabeth Stone and Michelle Saxton in particular. And many, many more – friends, neighbours, professionals and strangers who didn't need to help us, but did.

I should like to thank Di Speirs for suggesting that I approach my agent, to my agent Charlotte Robertson at Aitken Alexander, who gave me the best notes ever, and to my publisher George Morley, who has been a brilliant and patient editor of my mangled prose.

Above all, I should like to thank Jennie and Jessica and Lucy, because without them there would be no story and without their support, advice and love, I would never have been able to write mummy*daddy*.